Good Housekeeping
LOW CARB!

Mushroom Glazed Pork Chops (page 82)

Good Housekeeping
LOW CARB!
90 EASY & SATISFYING RECIPES

HEARST BOOKS

New York

HEARST BOOKS
New York

An Imprint of Sterling Publishing
387 Park Avenue South
New York, NY 10016

ISBN 978-1-61837-089-1

GOOD HOUSEKEEPING
Rosemary Ellis
EDITOR IN CHIEF

Courtney Murphy
CREATIVE DIRECTOR

Susan Westmoreland
FOOD DIRECTOR

Samantha B. Cassetty, M.S., R.D.
NUTRITION DIRECTOR

Sharon Franke
**KITCHEN APPLIANCES &
FOOD TECHNOLOGY DIRECTOR**

BOOK DESIGN: Memo Productions
PROJECT EDITOR: Sarah Scheffel
Photography Credits on page 158

The Good Housekeeping Cookbook Seal
guarantees that the recipes in this cookbook
meet the strict standards of the Good
Housekeeping Research Institute. The Institute
has been a source of reliable information and
a consumer advocate since 1900, and established
its seal of approval in 1909. Every recipe has
been triple-tested for ease, reliability, and
great taste.

Distributed in Canada by Sterling Publishing
c/o Canadian Manda Group, 165 Dufferin Street
Toronto, Ontario, Canada M6K 3H6

Distributed in the United Kingdom by
GMC Distribution Services
Castle Place, 166 High Street, Lewes, East Sussex,
England BN7 1XU

Distributed in Australia by Capricorn Link
(Australia) Pty. Ltd.
P.O. Box 704, Windsor, NSW 2756, Australia

For information about custom editions,
special sales, and premium and corporate
purchases, please contact Sterling Special
Sales at 800-805-5489 or
specialsales@sterlingpublishing.com.

Manufactured in China

2 4 6 8 10 9 7 5 3 1

www.sterlingpublishing.com

CONTENTS

Pot Roast Chili (page 65)

FOREWORD

We've been hearing regularly from readers who are looking for smart ways to cut back on carbohydrates (aka carbs), so we took up the challenge to provide delicious and diverse ways to keep the count down. Whenever we work on a book that features a lifestyle plan (check out our *Family Vegetarian Cookbook, Simple Vegan!, Easy Gluten-Free!,* and our *400 Calorie* series), I'm always happily surprised at our range of recipes. In these pages we've rounded up 90 satisfying main dishes that are big on flavor, easy to make, and contain just 20 grams of carbs (or less) per serving.

If you're already following a low-carb diet, you're probably familiar with the drill for meal-planning guidelines. But for newbies (and as a refresher for everyone), we review the basic nutrients you need for optimum health, offer tried-and-true tips for low-carb success, and invite you to use your slow cooker and nonstick skillet—they'll make meal prep a breeze! Whether you're controlling your carb intake to lose weight or to manage diabetes or another health issue, consider this book your ally.

Easy to prepare and light on your wallet, chicken and turkey are mainstays of a low-carb diet: Try our stir-fries, kabobs, roasts, and even a healthy turkey meatloaf. For red-meat lovers, we've included succulent steaks and chops, hearty stews, and salad plates.

Fish and shellfish are low in fat and high in protein, so we've included light and luscious recipes for everything from Ginger-Shallot Cod on Watercress to Shrimp and Tomato Summer Salad. Make it a habit to eat seafood at least once a week. And don't forget the power of eggs and vegetables: These make terrific low-carb breakfasts, lunches, and dinners. You'll love egg-centric dishes like Shrimp Egg Salad with Spring Peas and meatless mains like Roasted Eggplant Parmesan.

As always, every recipe is triple-tested and includes complete nutritional information. With *Good Housekeeping Low Carb!* in your kitchen, you'll never have to sacrifice flavor—or satisfaction!

SUSAN WESTMORELAND
Food Director, *Good Housekeeping*

INTRODUCTION

Welcome to *Good Housekeeping Low Carb!* Whether you're eating low carb to lose weight, controlling carbs because you're diabetic, or limiting carbs for other health reasons, enjoy our selection of tasty main dishes, plus suggestions for sides to round out your meals. All were chosen to keep you happy and satisfied while adhering to our nutrition department's low-carb guidelines: No more than 20 grams of carbs per serving.

Following a low-carb diet doesn't mean eliminating carbs from your diet! The goal is to reduce your total carb intake, limiting your intake of unhealthy carbs like refined white flour products and avoiding added sugar in favor of regulated portions of healthy carbs (see "Carbohydrates," opposite, for suggestions).

Here's how it works: Eating a meal high in carbohydrates raises the blood sugar level, which in turn raises the insulin level. When your insulin level is high, carbs are the main source of energy in your body. The low-carb theory is that when your insulin levels are low, your body uses a mixture of stored carbohydrates and fat as energy, thus promoting weight loss. A healthy diet will provide carbohydrates for your brain, help your body use stored fat as energy, and keep the muscle protein intact.

If losing weight is the goal, in addition to restricting carbs, be sure to watch your overall calorie count: Many experts agree that keeping track of calories consumed versus calories expended is the key to controlling weight. To help you do this, we've tagged all low-calorie recipes in the book with the following icon: ☺. This indicates main-dish meals, including a starch or fruit, that are 450 calories or less per serving, along with other main dishes that are 300 calories or less per serving. In addition, heart-healthy ♥, thirty-minutes-or-less ◔, make-ahead 🍴, and slow-cooker icons 🍲 will help you choose recipes that best suit your needs.

To make this book a lifesaver for busy cooks as dinnertime approaches, we've organized the chapters by main ingredient: chicken and turkey, beef and veal, pork and lamb, and seafood, plus a chapter on veggies, eggs, and cheese that includes many meatless mains. Many of these recipes are meals on their own. For those that aren't, we've provided quick and easy ideas for low-carb sides that we hope you'll find as inspiring as our entrées.

THE NUTRIENTS YOU NEED: THE BIG THREE

The U.S. Department of Agriculture (USDA) recommends that everyone eat a wide variety of foods to get the calories, nutrients, fiber, and vitamins they require for good health. Our bodies need three essential nutrients: carbohydrates, proteins, and fats.

Carbohydrates: The right kinds of carbohydrates are a key part of a well-balanced diet; they are the body's major source of energy, including fuel for the brain. "Good" carbohydrates include fruits, vegetables, legumes, and whole grains. Carbohydrates can be made up of dietary fiber, starch, or sugar. Those who follow a diet rich in dietary fiber have been shown to have a reduced risk of coronary heart disease, among other benefits, and research indicates that whole-grain eaters are thinner than people who eat few whole-grain foods.

The starch and sugar in carbohydrates supply the body with the energy it needs for normal functions. When carbohydrates are digested, they become blood sugar (glucose), which is then used as fuel in our bodies. In general, the less sugar you eat, the better. However, this doesn't include the naturally occurring sugar found in fruit, milk, or yogurt. The real culprit is the *added* sugar that comes from sweeteners, including white sugar, high-fructose corn syrup, dextrose, sucrose, fruit juice concentrate, and other sweeteners.

Proteins: The body needs protein to produce new body tissue. As anyone following a low-carb diet knows, proteins are also great for weight loss: They help keep you feeling full for hours after eating. Too much protein, however, is unhealthy; it can stress the kidneys, and if it comes from fatty meat, it is also filling you with saturated fat. For optimum health, you should eat a variety of protein-rich foods, in-

cluding seafood, lean meat and poultry, eggs, beans and lentils, soy products, and unsalted nuts and seeds. The latest USDA guidelines suggest that you eat more fish and non-meat protein; increase and vary your protein intake by substituting fish and shellfish (or beans, lentils, or tofu) in place of some of the meat and poultry you would typically eat.

Fats: The USDA guideline for fat consumption is 20 to 35 percent of your total daily calories, which is a wide range. However, much more important than the total fat is the amount of saturated and trans fat in your diet. Long-term studies suggest that when an excess of saturated fat is consumed, it raises your blood cholesterol level, increasing your risk of heart disease and stroke. Saturated fat is found naturally in foods, but it is especially concentrated in fatty animal-based foods, such as fatty red meat, butter, and chicken skin. If you're following a low-carb diet, you need to keep an especially close eye on your saturated fat intake. See "Proteins," above, for lower–fat proteins you should be sure to incorporate into your regular rotation.

Even worse than saturated fat is trans fat, which not only raises the LDL ("bad cholesterol") but also lowers the HDL ("good cholesterol"). It is formed by a process called hydrogenation, which turns oils into semisolids like margarine and shortening. Trans fats are used in

many packaged foods and baked goods. On the ingredients list, these oils appear as *partially hydrogenated* oils or *shortening* and are reflected in the trans-fat total on the Nutrition Facts label. It is important to keep your intake of trans fat low. Use canola or olive oil whenever possible and "0 trans" or "trans fat–free" margarine. Eliminate processed foods made with partially hydrogenated oils, and limit those made with butter or oils high in saturated fat (such as palm, palm kernel, and coconut).

Chicken Parm Stacks (page 20)

LOW-CARB SUCCESS

Although the rewards are motivating, sticking to a healthy diet that's low in carbohydrates can be challenging. Common pitfalls include loading up on red meat, cheese, and other items that are high in saturated fat and not eating enough vegetables, fruit, and whole grains that deliver the essential vitamins, phytonutrients, and dietary fiber you need for optimum health. And, of course, there's always the danger of cheating and binging on starchy potato dishes, white bread products, or sweets that contain little nutritional value. Here are our tips to help you stay the course!

Focus on lean meat, poultry, and seafood: To avoid consuming an excess of saturated fat, choose skinnier cuts of red meat like top-round roast, sirloin tip steak or brisket, lean ground beef, and pork tenderloin. When it comes to poultry, skinless boneless chicken breasts or turkey cutlets are always a smart choice. Remove the skin from chicken thighs and  whole chicken or turkey after cooking to retain all of the flavor without ingesting the extra fat. Fish and shellfish are naturally lean, making them great options for any meal. But don't skip oily fish like salmon and tuna: They contain omega-3s that are not only good for your heart and brain functioning, but aid in weight loss and management, too.

Don't forget whole grains: Brown rice, barley, quinoa, cornmeal, and more are all rich in dietary fiber, vitamins, and other nutrients. To keep carbs in check, try incorporating one-half a serving of whole grains into your meals: about ¼ cup cooked grains. Toss them with veggies, fresh herbs, and cheese, or make them part of your main dish by pairing them with a meat, poultry, or seafood entrée. You'll enjoy the benefits of whole-grain goodness while still sticking to your target carb count.

Avoid pasta pitfalls: You don't have to eliminate pasta altogether just because you're eating low carb. Simply reverse the usual proportions of pasta and sauce: Instead of a heaping plate of noodles topped with a little sauce, serve two-thirds meat and veggies with sauce tossed with one-third pasta (we recommend whole-grain noodles). That way, you can enjoy the comforts of pasta while avoiding the carb overload.

Another healthy solution: Try substituting ribbons of zucchini or yellow squash for noodles. Simply trim and discard the ends and peel long ribbons of squash with a vegetable peeler. Sauté the ribbons with a little olive oil and crushed garlic to create colorful vegetable "pasta" noodles.

Don't ban bread—just slice it thin: If you're craving a sandwich, try slicing whole-grain bread so thin that you are actually just eating one-third to one-half a serving—then enjoy your sandwich open face. You'll get your bread fix without blowing your carb count.

Eat fresh produce: Don't pass up colorful vegetables because you're saving your carbs for starchy white high-carb treats. To ensure satisfaction and good health, incorporate a wide range of fresh produce in all the colors of the rainbow. Think salads, veggie sides (steamed, grilled, sautéed, or roasted), fresh fruit platters, and crudités served with dip. Frozen vegetables are an easy and nutritious swap in a pinch.

Satisfy your sweet tooth—with fruit: The fructose, or sugar in fruit that gives it its sweetness, is low glycemic: It causes only a small rise in blood sugar levels if eaten in moderation in its natural form, the whole fruit. So, if you need a sweet fix, dip a strawberry or two in dark chocolate or create a yummy parfait by tossing a few slices of peach or mango in low-fat Greek yogurt—then sprinkle with toasted chopped nuts.

CHICKEN & TURKEY

One of the most adaptable proteins, poultry readily takes on a wide range of flavors and can be sautéed, roasted, braised, or grilled. Enjoy it in salads or sandwiches like our Turkey Meatball Lettuce Wraps, which cut carbs by replacing the bread with Boston lettuce leaves. Comfort food dishes like Coq au Vin are always satisfying, while grilled specialties like Beer Can Chicken delight a crowd.

┨ **KEY TO ICONS** ┠

⊘ 30 minutes or less   ☺ Low calorie   ♥ Heart healthy   ▤ Make ahead   ☎ Slow cooker

Roman Chicken Sauté with Artichokes (page 34)

TOMATO, SMOKED CHICKEN, AND MOZZARELLA SALAD

Prepare this refreshing main-dish salad in no time. It's best made in the summer, when vine-ripened tomatoes are plentiful.

TOTAL TIME: 15 MINUTES
MAKES: 4 MAIN-DISH SERVINGS

4	MEDIUM TOMATOES (1½ POUNDS)	2	TABLESPOONS EXTRA-VIRGIN OLIVE OIL
8	OUNCES FRESH MOZZARELLA CHEESE	2	TEASPOONS RED WINE VINEGAR
1	WHOLE BONE-IN SMOKED CHICKEN BREAST (1 POUND) OR 12 OUNCES DELI-SMOKED CHICKEN OR TURKEY	¼	TEASPOON SALT
2	TABLESPOONS SNIPPED FRESH CHIVES	2	PINCHES COARSELY GROUND BLACK PEPPER
¼	CUP THINLY SLICED FRESH BASIL LEAVES		

1 Thinly slice 3 tomatoes. Arrange overlapping slices of tomatoes in circle around edge of serving platter. Thinly slice half of mozzarella; cut each slice in half. Tuck sliced mozzarella here and there between tomato slices.

2 Cut remaining tomato and mozzarella into ½-inch chunks. Remove skin and bones from chicken and discard. Cut meat into ¾-inch chunks.

3 In large bowl, toss chunks of tomato, mozzarella, and chicken with chives, 2 tablespoons basil, 1 tablespoon oil, 1 teaspoon vinegar, ⅛ teaspoon salt, and pinch pepper.

4 Arrange chicken mixture in center of platter. Drizzle tomato and mozzarella slices with remaining 1 tablespoon oil and 1 teaspoon vinegar; sprinkle with remaining ⅛ teaspoon salt and pinch pepper. Top with remaining 2 tablespoons basil.

EACH SERVING: ABOUT 340 CALORIES | 26G PROTEIN | 16G CARBOHYDRATE | 22G TOTAL FAT (10G SATURATED) | 2G FIBER | 87MG CHOLESTEROL | 880MG SODIUM ♥ ☺

WATERCRESS AND PEACH SALAD WITH TURKEY

The addition of deli turkey (or ham, if you prefer) transforms this fresh and colorful summer salad into a meal.

TOTAL TIME: 20 MINUTES PLUS MARINATING

MAKES: 4 MAIN-DISH SERVINGS

2 TO 3 LIMES

½ TEASPOON DIJON MUSTARD

2 TABLESPOONS OLIVE OIL

½ TEASPOON SALT

¼ TEASPOON COARSELY GROUND BLACK PEPPER

4 RIPE LARGE PEACHES (2 POUNDS), PEELED, PITTED, AND CUT INTO WEDGES

2 BUNCHES WATERCRESS (7 TO 8 OUNCES EACH), TOUGH STEMS DISCARDED

8 OUNCES SLICED DELI TURKEY OR HAM, CUT CROSSWISE INTO ¼-INCH STRIPS

1 From limes, grate ½ teaspoon peel and squeeze 3 tablespoons juice.

2 In medium bowl, with wire whisk, mix ¼ teaspoon lime peel and 2 tablespoons lime juice with mustard, 1 tablespoon oil, ¼ teaspoon salt, and ⅛ teaspoon pepper. Gently stir in peaches; let stand 15 minutes.

3 Just before serving, in large bowl, toss watercress and turkey with remaining ¼ teaspoon lime peel, 1 tablespoon lime juice, 1 tablespoon oil, ¼ teaspoon salt, and ⅛ teaspoon pepper. Transfer watercress mixture to platter; top with peach mixture.

EACH SERVING: ABOUT 205 CALORIES | 20G PROTEIN | 17G CARBOHYDRATE | 7G TOTAL FAT (1G SATURATED) | 3G FIBER | 47MG CHOLESTEROL | 360MG SODIUM ☺ ♥

CURRIED CHICKEN WITH MANGO-CANTALOUPE SLAW

A sprightly slaw adds color and crunch to grilled chicken.

ACTIVE TIME: 25 MINUTES · **TOTAL TIME:** 35 MINUTES PLUS MARINATING

MAKES: 4 MAIN-DISH SERVINGS

---

2 TO 3 LIMES

1   CONTAINER (6 OUNCES) PLAIN LOW-FAT YOGURT

1   TEASPOON CURRY POWDER

1   TEASPOON GRATED, PEELED FRESH GINGER

1   TEASPOON SALT

¼   TEASPOON CRUSHED RED PEPPER

4   MEDIUM SKINLESS, BONELESS CHICKEN-BREAST HALVES (1¼ POUNDS)

½   SMALL CANTALOUPE, RIND REMOVED, CUT INTO 2" BY ¼" MATCHSTICK STRIPS (2 CUPS)

1   LARGE MANGO, PEELED AND CUT INTO 2" BY ¼" MATCHSTICK STRIPS (2 CUPS)

½   CUP LOOSELY PACKED FRESH CILANTRO LEAVES, CHOPPED

1   HEAD BOSTON LETTUCE

1 From 1 or 2 limes, grate ½ teaspoon peel and squeeze 2 tablespoons juice. In large bowl, with wire whisk, whisk 1 tablespoon lime juice and ¼ teaspoon lime peel with yogurt, curry powder, ginger, ¾ teaspoon salt, and ⅛ teaspoon crushed red pepper. Add chicken, turning to coat with marinade. Cover and let stand 15 minutes at room temperature or 30 minutes in refrigerator, turning occasionally.

2 Meanwhile, prepare slaw: In medium bowl, with rubber spatula, gently stir cantaloupe and mango with cilantro, 1 tablespoon lime juice, ¼ teaspoon lime peel, ¼ teaspoon salt, and ⅛ teaspoon crushed red pepper; set aside. Makes about 4 cups.

3 Prepare outdoor grill for direct grilling over medium heat. Grease grill rack. Remove chicken from marinade; discard marinade. Place chicken on hot rack. Cover and grill, 10 to 12 minutes, turning once, until instant-read thermometer registers 165°F. Transfer chicken to cutting board; cool slightly, then cut into long thin slices. Cut remaining lime into wedges.

4 To serve, arrange lettuce leaves on dinner plates; top with chicken and slaw. Garnish with lime wedges.

EACH SERVING CHICKEN WITH ½ CUP SLAW: ABOUT 255 CALORIES | 35G PROTEIN | 18G CARBOHYDRATE | 4G TOTAL FAT (1G SATURATED) | 2G FIBER | 92MG CHOLESTEROL | 480MG SODIUM ☺ ❤

CHICKEN PARM STACKS

Chicken Parmesan goes healthy with grilled, rather than breaded, chicken and fresh veggies. A sprinkling of whole-wheat bread crumbs adds crunch without a lot of carbs. For photo, see page 11.

ACTIVE TIME: 20 MINUTES · **TOTAL TIME:** 30 MINUTES
MAKES: 4 MAIN-DISH SERVINGS

1	SLICE WHOLE-WHEAT BREAD	1	POUND CHICKEN-BREAST CUTLETS
4	TEASPOONS OLIVE OIL	1	POUND YELLOW SQUASH, CUT INTO ½-INCH-THICK SLICES
¼	CUP PACKED FRESH FLAT-LEAF PARSLEY LEAVES	1	POUND RIPE TOMATOES, CUT INTO ½-INCH-THICK SLICES
1	CLOVE GARLIC	1	OUNCE PARMESAN CHEESE
⅜	TEASPOON SALT		BASIL LEAVES FOR GARNISH
⅜	TEASPOON GROUND BLACK PEPPER		

1 Arrange oven rack 6 inches from broiler heat source. Preheat broiler. Line 18" by 12" jelly-roll pan with foil. Preheat large ridged grill pan or prepare outdoor grill for direct grilling over medium-high heat.

2 Tear bread into large chunks. In food processor with knife blade attached, pulse bread into fine crumbs. In small bowl, combine bread crumbs with 1 teaspoon oil.

3 In food processor, combine parsley, garlic, ¼ teaspoon each salt and pepper, and remaining 1 tablespoon oil. Pulse until very finely chopped.

4 On large plate, rub half of parsley mixture all over chicken cutlets. Add chicken to hot grill pan or place on hot grill grate; cook 4 minutes. Turn chicken over and cook 3 to 4 minutes longer, until instant-read thermometer inserted into center of cutlet registers 165°F.

5 Meanwhile, arrange squash in prepared pan. Toss with remaining parsley mixture. Broil 7 to 9 minutes or until squash is tender and browned. Transfer squash to serving platter in single layer. Place chicken on top.

6 In same baking pan, arrange tomatoes in single layer. Divide crumb mixture evenly among tomatoes. Sprinkle with remaining ⅛ teaspoon each salt and pepper. Broil 30 seconds or until crumbs are golden brown.

7 Arrange tomato slices on top of chicken. With vegetable peeler, shave paper-thin slices of Parmesan over tomatoes. Garnish with basil.

EACH SERVING: ABOUT 250 CALORIES | 29G PROTEIN | 12G CARBOHYDRATE | 10G TOTAL FAT (3G SATURATED) | 3G FIBER | 69MG CHOLESTEROL | 415MG SODIUM ♥ ☺ ♥

TURKEY MEATBALL LETTUCE WRAPS

Lean turkey meatballs in lettuce cups get their savory zing from garlic, mint, and Asian fish sauce, while carrots add crunch. No grill? To cook the meatballs on a stovetop, use a grill pan and increase the cooking time to eight minutes.

ACTIVE TIME: 25 MINUTES · **TOTAL TIME:** 30 MINUTES PLUS SOAKING SKEWERS

MAKES: 4 MAIN-DISH SERVINGS

4	METAL OR BAMBOO SKEWERS (SEE BOX, PAGE 29)	2	GARLIC CLOVES, FINELY CHOPPED
3	LIMES	4	TEASPOONS SUGAR-FREE ASIAN FISH SAUCE (SEE TIP)
3	CUPS SHREDDED CARROTS	¾	TEASPOON GROUND BLACK PEPPER
½	CUP PACKED FRESH MINT LEAVES, THINLY SLICED	1	POUND LEAN (93%) GROUND TURKEY
		12	BOSTON LETTUCE LEAVES

1 If using bamboo skewers, soak them in hot water for at least 30 minutes. Prepare outdoor grill for direct grilling over medium-high heat.

2 From 2 limes, squeeze ¼ cup juice into small bowl. Cut remaining lime into wedges.

3 To lime juice, add carrots, ¼ cup mint, ¼ teaspoon garlic, 1 teaspoon fish sauce, and ¼ teaspoon pepper. Stir; let stand.

4 In large bowl, with hands, combine turkey with remaining 1 tablespoon fish sauce, ½ teaspoon pepper, ¼ cup mint, and garlic. Shape 1 tablespoon of mixture into meatball. Repeat with remaining mixture. Arrange on skewers, ½ inch apart; flatten slightly.

5 Grill meatballs 4 to 5 minutes or until grill marks appear and meat loses pink color throughout, turning occasionally.

6 Divide meatballs and carrot mixture among lettuce leaves. Serve with lime wedges.

TIP The "secret ingredient" in Southeast Asian cooking, Asian fish sauce is a thin, translucent, salty brown liquid extracted from salted, fermented fish. Red Boat Fish Sauce is sugar free; it's available online.

EACH SERVING: ABOUT 230 CALORIES | 27G PROTEIN | 15G CARBOHYDRATE | 7G TOTAL FAT (2G SATURATED) | 4G FIBER | 66MG CHOLESTEROL | 415MG SODIUM 🖤 ☺ 🖤

CHINESE FIVE-SPICE GRILLED CHICKEN

This quick and easy dish delivers lots of flavor from just a few ingredients. To keep the fat in check, remove the skin from the chicken before grilling. To make it a meal, serve with snow peas, fresh ginger, and garlic sautéed in light sesame oil—¾ cup contains 9 grams of carbs.

ACTIVE TIME: 10 MINUTES · **TOTAL TIME:** 35 MINUTES PLUS MARINATING

MAKES: 4 MAIN-DISH SERVINGS

¼ CUP DRY SHERRY

1 TABLESPOON ASIAN SESAME OIL

1 TEASPOON CHINESE FIVE-SPICE POWDER

¼ TEASPOON CAYENNE (GROUND RED) PEPPER

1 CHICKEN (3½ POUNDS), CUT INTO 8 PIECES, SKIN REMOVED FROM ALL BUT WINGS IF YOU LIKE

⅓ CUP SUGAR-FREE HOISIN SAUCE (SEE TIP)

1 TABLESPOON SOY SAUCE

1 TEASPOON SESAME SEEDS FOR GARNISH

1 In large bowl, whisk together sherry, sesame oil, five-spice powder, and cayenne pepper.

2 Add chicken to spice mixture and toss until evenly coated. Cover bowl and let stand 15 minutes at room temperature, turning chicken occasionally.

3 Prepare outdoor grill for direct grilling over medium heat.

4 Place chicken on hot grill rack. Cover grill and cook chicken, turning pieces once, until juices run clear when chicken is pierced with knife, 20 to 25 minutes. (Instant-read thermometer inserted into center of chicken pieces should register 165°F.) Remove chicken to platter as pieces are done.

5 In small bowl, mix hoisin and soy sauces. Brush sauce mixture all over chicken and return to grill. Cook until glazed, 4 to 5 minutes longer, turning once. Place chicken on same platter; sprinkle with sesame seeds.

TIP Steel's Rocky Mountain Hoisin Sauce is sugar-free; it's available online.

EACH SERVING WITHOUT SKIN: ABOUT 350 CALORIES | 41G PROTEIN | 10G CARBOHYDRATE 15G TOTAL FAT (4G SATURATED) | 0G FIBER | 121MG CHOLESTEROL | 595MG SODIUM

EACH SERVING WITH SKIN: ABOUT 580 CALORIES | 41G PROTEIN | 12G CARBOHYDRATE 39G TOTAL FAT (11G SATURATED) | 0G FIBER | 161MG CHOLESTEROL | 621MG SODIUM

BEER CAN CHICKEN WITH GINGER-JALAPEÑO SLAW

Here's a fun way to prepare grilled chicken, accompanied by a zippy Asian twist on coleslaw.

ACTIVE TIME: 15 MINUTES · **TOTAL TIME:** 1 HOUR 15 MINUTES PLUS STANDING
MAKES: 8 MAIN-DISH SERVINGS

BEER CAN CHICKEN

3 TABLESPOONS PAPRIKA

1 TABLESPOON SALT

2 TEASPOONS COARSELY GROUND BLACK PEPPER

1 TEASPOON ONION POWDER

1 TEASPOON GARLIC POWDER

1 TEASPOON CAYENNE (GROUND RED) PEPPER

2 CHICKENS (3½ POUNDS EACH), GIBLETS AND NECKS RESERVED FOR ANOTHER USE

2 CANS (12 OUNCES EACH) BEER

GINGER-JALAPEÑO SLAW

⅓ CUP RICE VINEGAR

2 TABLESPOONS OLIVE OIL

2 TEASPOONS GRATED, PEELED FRESH GINGER

½ TEASPOON SALT

2 JALAPEÑO CHILES, SEEDED AND MINCED

1 POUND GREEN CABBAGE, THINLY SLICED (6 CUPS)

½ POUND RED CABBAGE, THIINLY SLICED (3 CUPS)

3 MEDIUM CARROTS, PEELED AND FINELY SHREDDED (1½ CUPS)

2 GREEN ONIONS, THINLY SLICED

1 CUP THINLY SLICED KALE

1 To grill chicken: Prepare charcoal fire for indirect grilling with drip pan as manufacturer directs (see Tip), or preheat gas grill for indirect grilling over medium heat.

2 In small bowl, combine paprika, salt, black pepper, onion powder, garlic powder, and cayenne. Sprinkle 1 tablespoon spice mixture inside cavity of each chicken. Rub remaining spice mixture over outside of chickens.

3 Wipe beer cans clean. Open cans; pour ½ cup beer out of each can and reserve for another use. With can opener (church key style), make four additional holes in top of each can.

4 Set one partially filled beer can on flat surface. Hold one chicken upright, with opening of body cavity down, and slide chicken over top of can so can is inside cavity. Repeat with remaining chicken and can. With large spatula, transfer chickens, one at a time, to center of hot grill rack, keeping cans upright. (If using charcoal, place chickens over drip pan.) Spread out legs to balance chickens on rack.

5   Cover grill and cook chickens 1 hour to 1 hour 15 minutes. Temperature on instant-read thermometer inserted into thickest part of thigh, next to body (but not touching bone), should register 165°F when chicken is done.

6   Meanwhile, make slaw: In large bowl, with wire whisk, whisk vinegar, oil, ginger, salt, and jalapeños until blended. Add green and red cabbage, carrots, green onions, and kale; toss well to coat with dressing. Cover and refrigerate at least 1 hour to allow flavors to blend. Makes 8 cups.

7   With tongs and barbecue mitts, remove chickens and cans from grill, being careful not to spill beer. Let chicken stand 10 minutes before lifting from cans. Transfer chicken to platter or carving board; discard beer. Serve slaw alongside.

TIP   If you're using a charcoal grill, you'll need to keep the fire stoked by adding ten fresh charcoal briquettes to each side of the grill if more than one hour of cooking is required.

EACH SERVING CHICKEN WITH 1 CUP SLAW: ABOUT 420 CALORIES | 41G PROTEIN | 14G CARBOHYDRATE | 23G TOTAL FAT (6G SATURATED) | 4G FIBER | 112MG CHOLESTEROL 1,465MG SODIUM ☺

SUMMER SQUASH AND CHICKEN

Toss these wholesome ingredients on the grill for a simple, satisfying summer meal.

ACTIVE TIME: 15 MINUTES · **TOTAL TIME:** 25 MINUTES PLUS MARINATING
MAKES: 4 MAIN-DISH SERVINGS

---

1   LEMON

1   TABLESPOON OLIVE OIL

½   TEASPOON SALT

¼   TEASPOON COARSELY GROUND BLACK PEPPER

4   SKINLESS, BONELESS CHICKEN THIGHS (1¼ POUNDS)

4   MEDIUM YELLOW SUMMER SQUASH AND/OR ZUCCHINI (8 OUNCES EACH), EACH CUT LENGTHWISE INTO 4 WEDGES

¼   CUP SNIPPED FRESH CHIVES FOR GARNISH

1   From lemon, grate 1 tablespoon peel and squeeze 3 tablespoons juice. In medium bowl, with wire whisk, whisk together lemon peel and juice, oil, salt, and pepper; transfer 2 tablespoons to cup and set aside.

2   Add chicken to bowl with lemon marinade; cover and let stand 15 minutes at room temperature or 30 minutes in the refrigerator.

3   Meanwhile, prepare grill for direct grilling over medium heat.

4   Discard chicken marinade. Place chicken and squash on hot grill rack. Cover and grill until chicken loses pink color throughout and squash is tender and browned, 10 to 12 minutes, turning each piece over once and removing pieces as they are done. (Instant-read thermometer inserted into thickest part of thighs should register 165°F.)

5   Transfer chicken and squash to cutting board. Cut chicken into 1-inch-wide strips; cut each squash wedge crosswise in half.

6   To serve, on large platter, toss squash with reserved lemon-juice marinade, then toss with chicken and sprinkle with chives.

EACH SERVING: ABOUT 255 CALORIES | 29G PROTEIN | 8G CARBOHYDRATE | 8G TOTAL FAT (3G SATURATED) | 3G FIBER | 101MG CHOLESTEROL | 240MG SODIUM ☺ ♥

TURKEY KABOBS WITH GARDEN TOMATO JAM

Cut lean turkey breast into cubes, then marinate in a savory spice mixture. Serve the grilled kabobs with a quick dipping sauce of tomato and onion jam sweetened with raisins and orange juice. Round out the meal with a watercress and avocado salad tossed with orange juice and olive oil. It'll cost you less than 3 grams of carbs per cup.

ACTIVE TIME: 30 MINUTES · **TOTAL TIME:** 40 MINUTES PLUS MARINATING
MAKES: 6 MAIN-DISH SERVINGS

---

1   LARGE GARLIC CLOVE, CRUSHED WITH GARLIC PRESS

2   TABLESPOONS OLIVE OIL

1½ TEASPOONS CHILI POWDER

¾   TEASPOON PAPRIKA

1   TEASPOON SALT

¼   TEASPOON CAYENNE (GROUND RED) PEPPER

¼   TEASPOON GROUND BLACK PEPPER

2   POUNDS SKINLESS, BONELESS TURKEY BREAST, CUT INTO 1½-INCH CUBES

6   METAL OR BAMBOO SKEWERS (SEE OPPOSITE)

1   NAVEL ORANGE

1   SMALL ONION, CHOPPED

1   POUND PLUM TOMATOES, SEEDED AND CUT INTO ¼-INCH CUBES

⅓   CUP GOLDEN RAISINS

¼   CUP LOOSELY PACKED FRESH CILANTRO LEAVES, CHOPPED

1   In large resealable plastic bag, combine garlic, 1 tablespoon oil, chili powder, paprika, ¾ teaspoon salt, cayenne, and black pepper. Add turkey to bag, turning to coat with spice mixture. Seal bag, pressing out excess air. Place bag on plate; refrigerate at least 15 minutes or up to 1 hour.

2   Meanwhile, if using bamboo skewers, soak them in hot water at least 30 minutes. Prepare outdoor grill for direct grilling over medium heat.

3   While grill preheats and skewers soak, prepare garden tomato jam: From orange, grate 1 teaspoon peel and squeeze ¼ cup juice. In 10-inch skillet, heat remaining 1 tablespoon oil over medium-low heat. Add onion and cook, stirring occasionally, until golden, about 5 minutes. Add tomatoes, raisins, remaining ¼ teaspoon salt, and orange peel and juice. Increase heat to medium-high; cook until tomatoes soften and liquid evaporates, about 6 minutes. Remove skillet from heat. Makes about 1½ cups.

SKEWER KNOW-HOW

Chunks of turkey, chicken, steak, or vegetables—whatever you're skewering, follow these tips for kabob success.

If you use metal skewers, look for the kind that are twisted or square—not round. Food twirls around when you try to turn it on a round skewer. (Wooden and skinny bamboo skewers aren't slippery, so their round shape is no problem.)

Before using wooden or bamboo skewers, soak them in hot water for at least thirty minutes so they won't burn when exposed to the grill's heat and flames.

For even cooking, don't jam foods up against each other when you assemble the kabob—leave a little space between them on the skewer.

Use two parallel skewers for unwieldy items, like thick, large slices of onion.

Combine foods with similar cooking times on the same skewer.

4 Thread turkey onto six skewers. Place skewers on hot grill rack. Grill, turning occasionally, until turkey loses pink color throughout, about 10 minutes. Stir chopped cilantro into jam; serve with turkey.

EACH SERVING TURKEY WITH ¼ CUP JAM: ABOUT 250 CALORIES | 35G PROTEIN
14G CARBOHYDRATE | 6G TOTAL FAT (1G SATURATED) | 2G FIBER | 94MG CHOLESTEROL
460MG SODIUM ☺

LEMON-MINT CHICKEN CUTLETS ON WATERCRESS

The tang of lemon and the peppery punch of watercress make this a refreshing choice on a hot summer night. Another plus is that these thin cutlets will cook up in just a few minutes.

ACTIVE TIME: 15 MINUTES · **TOTAL TIME:** 20 MINUTES
MAKES: 4 MAIN-DISH SERVINGS

1¼ POUNDS THINLY SLICED SKINLESS, BONELESS CHICKEN BREASTS

2 LEMONS

2 TABLESPOONS OLIVE OIL

2 TABLESPOONS CHOPPED FRESH MINT, PLUS MORE FOR GARNISH

½ TEASPOON SALT

½ TEASPOON COARSELY GROUND BLACK PEPPER

1 BAG (4 OUNCES) BABY WATERCRESS

1 Heat large ridged grill pan over medium-high heat until hot, or prepare outdoor grill for direct grilling over medium-high heat.

2 Pound chicken to uniform 1/4-inch thickness if necessary.

3 From lemons, grate 1 tablespoon plus 11/2 teaspoons peel and squeeze 3 tablespoons juice. In large bowl, mix lemon peel and juice, oil, 2 tablespoons mint, salt, and pepper until dressing is blended.

4 Reserve 1/4 cup dressing. In large bowl, toss chicken with remaining dressing. Place chicken on hot grill pan or rack and cook until juices run clear when breast is pierced with tip of knife, 4 to 5 minutes, turning over once.

5 To serve, toss watercress with reserved dressing and top with chicken. Sprinkle with additional mint for garnish.

EACH SERVING: ABOUT 225 CALORIES | 34G PROTEIN | 2G CARBOHYDRATE | 9G TOTAL FAT (1G SATURATED) | 82MG CHOLESTEROL | 375MG SODIUM ❤ ☺ ♥

PEANUT CHICKEN STIR-FRY

Delight your family by preparing this popular Chinese restaurant dish at home. Using instant rice, chicken tenders, and prepackaged broccoli florets, you'll have it on the table in a flash.

ACTIVE TIME: 10 MINUTES · **TOTAL TIME:** 20 MINUTES

MAKES: 4 MAIN-DISH SERVINGS

1   CUP INSTANT BROWN RICE

1   CUP CANNED CHICKEN BROTH

2   TABLESPOONS SOY SAUCE

1   TABLESPOON CORNSTARCH

2   TEASPOONS VEGETABLE OIL

1   POUND CHICKEN-BREAST TENDERS, EACH CUT LENGTHWISE IN HALF

1   PACKAGE (12 OUNCES) BROCCOLI FLORETS

1   SMALL RED PEPPER, CUT INTO 1-INCH PIECES

1   SMALL ONION, CUT IN HALF AND SLICED

1   TEASPOON GRATED, PEELED FRESH GINGER

½   CUP UNSALTED ROASTED PEANUTS

1   TEASPOON ASIAN SESAME OIL

1   Prepare rice as label directs.

2   Meanwhile, in small bowl, whisk together broth, soy sauce, and cornstarch until smooth.

3   In nonstick 12-inch skillet, heat oil over medium. Add chicken and cook, stirring frequently (stir-frying), until it just loses pink color throughout, 4 to 5 minutes. Transfer chicken to bowl.

4   To same skillet, add broccoli, red pepper, onion, ginger, and ¼ cup broth mixture. Cover skillet and cook, stirring occasionally, until vegetables are tender-crisp, about 3 minutes. Stir in remaining broth mixture and add chicken with any juices to skillet; heat to boiling over medium-high. Boil until mixture has thickened slightly, about 1 minute. Remove skillet from heat; stir in peanuts and sesame oil.

5   To serve, spoon rice onto four dinner plates; top with chicken mixture.

EACH SERVING: ABOUT 265 CALORIES | 25G PROTEIN | 20G CARBOHYDRATE | 10G TOTAL FAT (1G SATURATED) | 44MG CHOLESTEROL | 560MG SODIUM

CHICKEN WITH PEARS AND MARSALA

Fresh pears and a wine sauce spiked with sage transform basic chicken breasts into an elegant main course. Serve with steamed broccoli florets as shown in photo—just 6 grams of carbs per ½ cup serving.

ACTIVE TIME: 10 MINUTES · **TOTAL TIME:** 25 MINUTES

MAKES: 4 MAIN-DISH SERVINGS

1 TEASPOON VEGETABLE OIL	¾ CUP CANNED CHICKEN BROTH
4 SMALL SKINLESS, BONELESS CHICKEN-BREAST HALVES (1 POUND)	½ CUP DRY MARSALA WINE
¼ TEASPOON SALT	1 TABLESPOON CORNSTARCH
⅛ TEASPOON GROUND BLACK PEPPER	2 TEASPOONS CHOPPED FRESH SAGE LEAVES
2 BOSC OR ANJOU PEARS, EACH PEELED, CORED, AND QUARTERED	

1 In nonstick 10-inch skillet, heat oil over medium heat. Add chicken; sprinkle with salt and pepper. Cook, turning once, until chicken loses pink color throughout, 10 to 12 minutes. (Instant-read thermometer inserted horizontally into center of breast should register 165°F.) Transfer to plate; keep warm.

2 To skillet, add pears and cook until browned on all sides, 3 to 5 minutes. Meanwhile, in cup, whisk broth, wine, cornstarch, and sage until blended.

3 Carefully add broth mixture to skillet; boil 1 minute to thicken slightly. Return chicken with any juices to skillet; heat through.

EACH SERVING: ABOUT 195 CALORIES | 27G PROTEIN | 12G CARBOHYDRATE | 3G TOTAL FAT (1G SATURATED) | 66MG CHOLESTEROL | 410MG SODIUM 💚 ☺ 🖤

ROMAN CHICKEN SAUTÉ WITH ARTICHOKES

This light and tangy chicken dish, studded with sweet grape tomatoes and garlicky artichoke hearts, is served over a bed of spicy arugula. For photo, see page 14.

ACTIVE TIME: 15 MINUTES · **TOTAL TIME:** 30 MINUTES
MAKES: 6 MAIN-DISH SERVINGS

1¼ POUNDS CHICKEN-BREAST TENDERS, EACH CUT CROSSWISE IN HALF, THEN CUT LENGTHWISE IN HALF

¼ TEASPOON SALT

¼ TEASPOON GROUND BLACK PEPPER

1 TABLESPOON OLIVE OIL

2 GARLIC CLOVES, THINLY SLICED

1 CAN (13 TO 14 OUNCES) ARTICHOKE HEARTS, DRAINED, EACH CUT INTO QUARTERS

½ CUP DRY WHITE WINE

½ CUP CANNED CHICKEN BROTH

1 PINT GRAPE TOMATOES

1 TEASPOON GRATED FRESH LEMON PEEL, PLUS ADDITIONAL FOR GARNISH

1 BAG (5 TO 6 OUNCES) BABY ARUGULA

1 Sprinkle chicken with salt and pepper on all sides. In 12-inch skillet, heat 2 teaspoons oil over medium-high heat until very hot. Add chicken and cook, stirring occasionally, 8 minutes or until browned on the outside and no longer pink inside. With slotted spoon, transfer chicken to bowl.
2 To same skillet, add remaining 1 teaspoon oil. Reduce heat to medium and add garlic; cook 30 seconds or until golden. Stir in artichokes, and cook 3 to 4 minutes or until browned. Stir in wine and cook 1 minute over medium-high heat.
3 Add chicken broth and tomatoes; cover and cook 2 to 3 minutes or until most tomatoes burst. Remove skillet from heat. Return chicken to skillet; stir in lemon peel until combined. Arrange arugula on platter; top with sautéed chicken mixture. Garnish chicken with remaining lemon peel.

EACH SERVING: ABOUT 165 CALORIES | 25G PROTEIN | 7G CARBOHYDRATE | 4G TOTAL FAT (1G SATURATED) | 55MG CHOLESTEROL | 330MG SODIUM ◔ ☺ ♥

CHICKEN NOODLE SOUP

You can whip up this homey chicken and vegetable soup in thirty minutes. We used tiny bow-tie pasta to keep the carbs in check.

ACTIVE TIME: 15 MINUTES · **TOTAL TIME:** 30 MINUTES

MAKES: 8 CUPS OR 4 MAIN-DISH SERVINGS

1 LARGE LEEK (8 OUNCES)	½ CUP SMALL BOW-TIE PASTA
1 TABLESPOON OLIVE OIL	½ TEASPOON SALT
2 CARROTS, EACH PEELED, HALVED LENGTHWISE, AND CUT CROSSWISE INTO ¼-INCH-THICK SLICES	⅛ TEASPOON GROUND BLACK PEPPER
	3 CUPS WATER
1 CELERY STALK, THINLY SLICED	12 OUNCES SKINLESS, BONELESS CHICKEN-BREAST HALVES, CUT CROSSWISE INTO VERY THIN SLICES
¼ TEASPOON DRIED THYME	
1 BAY LEAF	
1 CAN (14½ OUNCES) CHICKEN BROTH	

1 Cut off root and leaf ends from leek. Discard any tough outer leaves. Cut leek lengthwise into ¼-inch-thick slices. Place in bowl of cold water and swish to remove any sand. With hands, transfer leek pieces to colander to drain. Repeat process, changing water several times until all sand is removed. Drain and set aside.

2 In 4-quart saucepan, heat oil over medium-high heat until hot. Add leek, carrots, celery, thyme, and bay leaf; cook until leek wilts and vegetables are tender-crisp, 5 to 7 minutes.

3 Add broth, pasta, salt, pepper, and water; heat to boiling over high heat. Reduce heat to medium-low; simmer, covered, until pasta is just cooked, 5 minutes. Increase heat to medium; add chicken pieces and cook, uncovered, until chicken loses pink color throughout, 3 minutes. Discard bay leaf before serving.

EACH SERVING: ABOUT 220 CALORIES | 23G PROTEIN | 17G CARBOHYDRATE | 6G TOTAL FAT (1G SATURATED) | 2G FIBER | 63MG CHOLESTEROL | 800MG SODIUM

COQ AU VIN

This classic one-dish meal—chicken and assorted vegetables stewed in red wine—is a French bistro favorite. Our irresistible version contains just 13 grams of carbs per serving.

ACTIVE TIME: 1 HOUR 15 MINUTES · **TOTAL TIME:** 1 HOUR 55 MINUTES
MAKES: 6 MAIN-DISH SERVINGS

4 SLICES BACON, CUT INTO ½-INCH PIECES	1 PACKAGE (12 OUNCES) MUSHROOMS, EACH CUT IN HALF OR INTO QUARTERS IF LARGE
4 POUNDS BONE-IN CHICKEN PARTS (THIGHS, DRUMSTICKS, AND/OR BREASTS), SKIN REMOVED	2 TABLESPOONS BUTTER OR MARGARINE
½ TEASPOON SALT	3 TABLESPOONS ALL-PURPOSE FLOUR
¼ TEASPOON COARSELY GROUND PEPPER	1½ CUPS DRY RED WINE
1 SMALL ONION, FINELY CHOPPED	1 CUP CHICKEN BROTH
1 CARROT, PEELED AND FINELY CHOPPED	2 TABLESPOONS TOMATO PASTE
1 CELERY STALK, FINELY CHOPPED	2 BAY LEAVES
20 PEARL ONIONS (5 OUNCES), SOAKED IN WARM WATER AND PEELED	½ CUP LOOSELY PACKED FRESH PARSLEY LEAVES AND STEMS, CHOPPED, FOR GARNISH

1 Preheat oven to 325°F. In 5-quart Dutch oven, cook bacon over medium heat until browned. With slotted spoon, transfer bacon to paper-towel-lined plate to drain.

2 Sprinkle chicken with salt and pepper. To bacon fat in Dutch oven, add half of chicken and cook over medium-high heat until browned on all sides, 10 minutes. With slotted spoon, transfer chicken to large bowl. Repeat with remaining chicken.

3 To same Dutch oven, add chopped onion, carrot, and celery; cook, stirring occasionally, until vegetables are tender, 10 minutes. With slotted spoon, transfer to bowl with chicken. Add pearl onions and mushrooms to Dutch oven and cook, stirring occasionally, until browned, 8 minutes. Transfer to bowl with chicken.

4 In same Dutch oven, melt butter. Add flour and cook, stirring frequently, 2 minutes. With wire whisk, whisk in wine until smooth. Stir in broth and tomato paste. Heat to boiling, whisking frequently; boil 2 minutes.

5 Return chicken, vegetables, and three-fourths of bacon to Dutch oven. Add bay leaves; heat to boiling. Cover Dutch oven and bake until chicken loses pink color throughout, 40 to 45 minutes, turning chicken pieces once. (Instant-read thermometer inserted into center of chicken pieces, but not touching bone, should register 165°F.)

6 To serve, discard bay leaves. Skim and discard fat. Transfer stew to large serving bowl; sprinkle with parsley and remaining bacon.

EACH SERVING: ABOUT 330 CALORIES | 36G PROTEIN | 13G CARBOHYDRATE | 14G TOTAL FAT (6G SATURATED) | 3G FIBER | 108MG CHOLESTEROL | 573MG SODIUM ☺ 🍲

HEALTHY MAKEOVER TURKEY MEATLOAF

To enjoy the comforts of meatloaf without all the carbs and fat, try this leaner version. Pair with mashed cauliflower instead of potatoes. It delivers the same creaminess for just 2½ grams of carbs per ½ cup serving.

ACTIVE TIME: 15 MINUTES · **TOTAL TIME:** 1 HOUR 10 MINUTES
MAKES: 8 MAIN-DISH SERVINGS

- 1   TABLESPOON OLIVE OIL
- 2   MEDIUM STALKS CELERY, FINELY CHOPPED
- 1   SMALL ONION, FINELY CHOPPED
- 1   GARLIC CLOVE, CRUSHED WITH GARLIC PRESS
- 2   POUNDS LEAN GROUND TURKEY
- ¾   CUP FRESH WHOLE-WHEAT BREAD CRUMBS (FROM 1½ SLICES BREAD)

- ⅓   CUP SKIM MILK
- 1   TABLESPOON WORCESTERSHIRE SAUCE
- 2   LARGE EGG WHITES
- ½   CUP SUGAR-FREE KETCHUP (SEE TIP)
- ½   TEASPOON SALT
- ½   TEASPOON COARSELY GROUND BLACK PEPPER
- 1   TABLESPOON DIJON MUSTARD

1   Preheat oven to 350°F.

2   In nonstick 12-inch skillet, heat oil over medium heat. Add celery and onion and cook until vegetables are tender, about 10 minutes, stirring occasionally. Add garlic and cook 1 minute. Transfer vegetables to large bowl; cool slightly.

3   To bowl with vegetables, add turkey, bread crumbs, milk, Worcestershire, egg whites, ¼ cup ketchup, salt, and pepper; mix with hands until well combined but not overmixed. In cup, mix Dijon and remaining ¼ cup ketchup.

4   In 13" by 9" metal baking pan, shape meat mixture into 9" by 5" loaf. Spread ketchup mixture over top of loaf. Bake meatloaf until instant-read thermometer inserted in center reaches 160°F, 55 to 60 minutes. (Temperature will rise to 165°F upon standing.)

5   Let meatloaf stand 10 minutes before removing from pan to set juices for easier slicing. Transfer meatloaf to platter and cut into slices to serve.

TIP   For sugar-free ketchup, try Schumann's; for reduced-sugar, opt for Heinz.

EACH SERVING: ABOUT 230 CALORIES | 25G PROTEIN | 7G CARBOHYDRATE | 11G TOTAL FAT (3G SATURATED) | 1G FIBER | 80MG CHOLESTEROL | 500MG SODIUM ☺ 🧺

PANKO-MUSTARD CHICKEN

This recipe for oven-baked chicken couldn't be simpler—or more delicious. The breasts are brushed with a zippy mustard mixture and then coated in Japanese-style bread crumbs, which become brown and crispy in the oven. Serve with asparagus stir-fried in light sesame oil and garlic and finished with a sprinkle of soy sauce and sesame seeds. A half cup of stir-fry adds just 3 grams of carbs to the meal.

ACTIVE TIME: 15 MINUTES · **TOTAL TIME:** 30 MINUTES

MAKES: 4 MAIN-DISH SERVINGS

---

1 SHALLOT, MINCED	½ CUP PANKO (JAPANESE-STYLE BREAD CRUMBS)
2 TABLESPOONS BUTTER OR MARGARINE	4 MEDIUM SKINLESS, BONELESS CHICKEN-BREAST HALVES (1¼ POUNDS)
2 TABLESPOONS DIJON MUSTARD WITH SEEDS	¼ TEASPOON SALT
2 TEASPOONS CHOPPED FRESH TARRAGON	

1 Preheat oven to 475°F.

2 In small microwave-safe bowl, place shallot and 2 teaspoons butter. Heat in microwave oven on High 1 minute to cook shallot slightly. Stir in mustard and tarragon.

3 In another small microwave-safe bowl, place remaining 4 teaspoons butter. Heat in microwave oven on High until melted, 15 to 20 seconds. Stir in panko until mixed.

4 Arrange chicken breasts in 15½" by 10½" jelly-roll pan; sprinkle with salt. Spread mustard mixture evenly over breasts; top with panko mixture, patting on gently. Bake in top third of oven until chicken loses pink color throughout, 12 to 15 minutes. (Instant-read thermometer inserted horizontally into center of breasts should register 165°F.)

EACH SERVING: ABOUT 270 CALORIES | 35G PROTEIN | 7G CARBOHYDRATE | 10G TOTAL FAT (5G SATURATED) | 0G FIBER | 107MG CHOLESTEROL | 383MG SODIUM ♡ ☺ ♥

PROSCIUTTO-WRAPPED TURKEY ROULADE

Elegant slices of juicy white meat, encircled in prosciutto and laced with herbs, rely on a simple roll-and-wrap technique. Add on a side of garlicky greens, if you like.

ACTIVE TIME: 30 MINUTES · **TOTAL TIME:** 2 HOURS
MAKES: 8 MAIN-DISH SERVINGS

1   LEMON

1   CUP PACKED FRESH FLAT-LEAF PARSLEY LEAVES

6   CLOVES GARLIC, PEELED

3   TABLESPOONS FRESH SAGE LEAVES

2   TABLESPOONS FRESH ROSEMARY LEAVES

1   TABLESPOON FENNEL SEEDS

½   TEASPOON SALT

¼   TEASPOON FRESHLY GROUND BLACK PEPPER

1   WHOLE BONELESS TURKEY BREAST (4 TO 5 POUNDS; SEE TIP), SKIN REMOVED

6   THICK SLICES PROSCIUTTO (5 OUNCES; SEE TIP)

2   LARGE RED ONIONS (8 TO 10 OUNCES EACH), PEELED AND CUT INTO ½-INCH-THICK ROUNDS

1   TABLESPOON CANOLA OIL

1   CUP LOWER-SODIUM CHICKEN BROTH

1   Preheat oven to 375°F. From lemon, grate 1 teaspoon peel; transfer to food processor. Into small bowl, squeeze 1 tablespoon juice; set aside.

2   To food processor, add parsley, garlic, sage, rosemary, fennel seeds, salt, and pepper. Pulse until finely chopped. Transfer to medium bowl.

3   Place turkey on large cutting board, smooth side down. On left breast, cut along right side of tenderloin to separate from breast without cutting tenderloin off completely. Fold tenderloin back until flat but still attached to breast along left side. Repeat on right breast, cutting along left side of tenderloin and folding back. Cover surface of turkey with 2 large sheets plastic wrap. Using flat side of meat mallet or heavy rolling pin, pound turkey until about ¾ inch thick all over. Remove and discard plastic wrap.

4   Spread three-quarters of herb mixture in even layer on breast. Starting with short side, roll breast in jelly-roll fashion. Place seam side down.

5   Rub outside of rolled turkey with remaining herb mixture. Cover top with prosciutto slices, overlapping slightly and tucking ends underneath turkey. Using 16-inch pieces of kitchen string, tie turkey tightly in 2-inch intervals. (Turkey can be wrapped tightly in plastic wrap and refrigerated overnight.)

6 Arrange onion rounds in single layer on bottom of medium roasting pan (14" by 10"). Place turkey on onions and brush both with oil. Pour broth into pan. Roast for 1½ to 2 hours or until instant read thermometer inserted into center of turkey registers 165°F. If pan seems dry after 45 minutes, add 1 cup water.

7 With tongs, transfer turkey to cutting board and onions to serving platter. Cover turkey loosely with foil. Place roasting pan on burner. Heat to boiling on medium-high; whisk in reserved 1 tablespoon lemon juice. (If liquid in pan is minimal and tastes too salty, add ½ cup water along with lemon juice.) Boil 3 to 5 minutes or until reduced slightly, whisking occasionally. Slice turkey; place on platter with onions. Drizzle turkey with reduced pan juices.

TIP For easier prep, ask your butcher to butterfly and pound the turkey breast for you so you can skip step 3. For easier wrapping, we used slightly thicker (not paper-thin) slices of prosciutto.

EACH SERVING: ABOUT 340 CALORIES | 62G PROTEIN | 8G CARBOHYDRATE | 5G TOTAL FAT (1G SATURATED) | 2G FIBER | 155MG CHOLESTEROL | 795MG SODIUM ♥

BEEF & VEAL

There's nothing as satisfying as tucking into a juicy steak. You'll especially relish our Pepper-Crusted Filet Mignon and Skirt Steak with Chimichurri Sauce. Or add vegetables to the mix and enjoy sliced steak in one of our stir-fries or salads, including Tangerine Beef Stir-Fry and, our twist on a classic, Grilled Steak Caesar Salad. Veal is an often-overlooked option; we encourage you to try sweet and tender cutlets in our Lemony Veal and Baby Artichokes recipe—it's delicious!

KEY TO ICONS

⬇ 30 minutes or less   ☺ Low calorie   ♥ Heart healthy   ▭ Make ahead   ▭ Slow cooker

Braciole with Grape Tomatoes (page 67)

LIGHTER BEEF AND BROCCOLI

Here's a streamlined version of the popular Chinese entrée—it's almost as quick as ordering takeout.

ACTIVE TIME: 25 MINUTES · TOTAL TIME: 40 MINUTES
MAKES: 4 MAIN-DISH SERVINGS

---

1 LARGE BUNCH BROCCOLI (1½ POUNDS)

1 POUND BEEF TENDERLOIN STEAKS, TRIMMED AND CUT INTO ⅛-INCH-THICK STRIPS

3 GARLIC CLOVES, CRUSHED WITH GARLIC PRESS

1 TABLESPOON GRATED, PEELED FRESH GINGER

¼ TEASPOON CRUSHED RED PEPPER

1 TEASPOON OLIVE OIL

¾ CUP CHICKEN BROTH

3 TABLESPOONS SOY SAUCE

1 TABLESPOON CORNSTARCH

½ TEASPOON ASIAN SESAME OIL

1 Cut broccoli florets into 1½-inch pieces. Peel broccoli stems and cut on a diagonal into ¼-inch-thick slices.

2 In nonstick 12-inch skillet, heat ½ *inch water* to boiling over medium heat. Add broccoli and cook, uncovered, until tender-crisp, 3 minutes. Drain broccoli and set aside. Wipe skillet dry.

3 In medium bowl, toss beef with garlic, ginger, and crushed red pepper. Add ½ teaspoon olive oil to skillet and heat over medium heat until hot but not smoking. Add half of beef mixture and cook, stirring quickly and frequently, until beef just loses pink color throughout, 2 to 3 minutes. Transfer beef to plate. Repeat with remaining ½ teaspoon olive oil and beef mixture.

4 In cup, mix broth, soy sauce, cornstarch, and sesame oil until blended. Return beef to skillet. Stir in cornstarch mixture; heat to boiling. Cook, stirring, until sauce thickens slightly, 1 minute. Add broccoli and toss to coat.

EACH SERVING: ABOUT 245 CALORIES | 28G PROTEIN | 10G CARBOHYDRATE | 11G TOTAL FAT (3G SATURATED) | 3G FIBER | 57MG CHOLESTEROL | 1,010MG SODIUM ☺

TANGERINE BEEF STIR-FRY

A mélange of broccoli, tangerines, and red pepper ensures that this stir-fry is as colorful as it is delicious.

ACTIVE TIME: 20 MINUTES · TOTAL TIME: 35 MINUTES

MAKES: 4 MAIN-DISH SERVINGS

---

3   TANGERINES (1½ POUNDS)

¼   CUP DRY SHERRY

2   TABLESPOONS SUGAR-FREE HOISIN OR TERIYAKI SAUCE (SEE TIP)

2   TABLESPOONS CORNSTARCH

2   TABLESPOONS SOY SAUCE

1   BEEF FLANK STEAK (1 POUND), CUT CROSSWISE INTO ⅛-INCH-THICK SLICES

5   TEASPOONS VEGETABLE OIL

1   BAG (12 OUNCES) BROCCOLI FLORETS

1   RED PEPPER, THINLY SLICED

1   TABLESPOON PEELED, GRATED FRESH GINGER

1   With vegetable peeler, remove peel from 1 tangerine. With small knife, remove any white pith from peel; slice peel very thinly and set aside. Squeeze ½ cup juice from tangerines; stir in sherry and hoisin sauce and set aside. In medium bowl, combine cornstarch, soy sauce, and steak; set aside.

2   In nonstick 12-inch skillet, heat 1 teaspoon oil over medium heat until very hot. Add broccoli, red pepper, ginger, and tangerine peel to skillet and cook 3 to 4 minutes, stirring, or until vegetables are tender-crisp. Transfer to large bowl.

3   In same skillet, heat 2 teaspoons oil over medium heat; add half of beef and cook 2 to 3 minutes, stirring, or until lightly browned. Transfer to bowl with broccoli mixture. Repeat with remaining 2 teaspoons oil and beef.

4   Add juice mixture to skillet and heat to boiling; boil 1 minute. Return vegetables and beef to skillet; heat through.

TIP   Seal Sama and Organicville brands make sugar-free teriyaki sauces. They're available online.

EACH SERVING: ABOUT 350 CALORIES | 26G PROTEIN | 17G CARBOHYDRATE | 18G TOTAL FAT (6G SATURATED) | 4G FIBER | 59MG CHOLESTEROL | 525MG SODIUM ☺

PAN-FRIED STEAK WITH SPINACH AND TOMATOES

Juicy top loin steaks topped with a garlicky lemon rub are complemented by quickly sautéed vegetables.

ACTIVE TIME: 15 MINUTES · TOTAL TIME: 30 MINUTES
MAKES: 4 MAIN-DISH SERVINGS

1 LARGE GARLIC CLOVE, CRUSHED WITH GARLIC PRESS

1 TEASPOON FRESHLY GRATED LEMON PEEL

½ TEASPOON SALT

½ TEASPOON COARSELY GROUND BLACK PEPPER

2 BONELESS BEEF TOP LOIN OR RIB-EYE STEAKS, ¾ INCH THICK (10 OUNCES EACH), TRIMMED

1 TEASPOON OLIVE OIL

½ CUP CANNED CHICKEN BROTH

1 TEASPOON CORNSTARCH

1 CUP GRAPE TOMATOES OR CHERRY TOMATOES, EACH CUT IN HALF

1 BAG (10 OUNCES) PREWASHED SPINACH, TOUGH STEMS TRIMMED

1   In cup, with fork, blend garlic, lemon peel, salt, and pepper. Spread garlic mixture on both sides of steaks.

2   In nonstick 12-inch skillet, heat oil over medium heat until hot. Add steaks and cook until medium-rare, 5 to 6 minutes per side, or to desired doneness. (Instant-read thermometer inserted horizontally into center of steak should register 145°F.) Transfer steaks to plate; keep warm.

3   In cup, mix broth and cornstarch. To same skillet, add broth mixture, tomatoes, and spinach. Heat to boiling over medium-high heat and cook, stirring, until spinach wilts, 1 to 2 minutes. Cut each steak in half; serve with spinach mixture.

EACH SERVING: ABOUT 350 CALORIES | 30G PROTEIN | 3G CARBOHYDRATE | 24G TOTAL FAT (9G SATURATED) | 92MG CHOLESTEROL | 540MG SODIUM ☺

STEAK WITH SHALLOT–RED WINE SAUCE

Make this steak and its sauce in a single pan in just thirty minutes. This would be delicious with a side of sautéed escarole tossed with golden raisins and toasted pinenuts. Limit the raisins to 1 tablespoon and the nuts to ½ tablespoon per serving for a total carb count of 12 grams.

ACTIVE TIME: 5 MINUTES · TOTAL TIME: 30 MINUTES
MAKES: 4 MAIN-DISH SERVINGS

1 TEASPOON VEGETABLE OIL	¼ TEASPOON COARSELY GROUND BLACK PEPPER
2 BONELESS BEEF RIB-EYE STEAKS, ¾ INCH THICK (12 OUNCES EACH)	¼ CUP FINELY CHOPPED SHALLOTS
1 TEASPOON BUTTER OR MARGARINE	1 CUP DRY RED WINE
½ TEASPOON SALT	

1 In 12-inch skillet, heat oil over medium-high heat until very hot.

2 Meanwhile, pat steaks dry with paper towels.

3 Add butter to skillet. Add steaks; sprinkle with salt and pepper and cook 4 to 5 minutes per side for medium-rare or to desired doneness. (Instant-read thermometer inserted horizontally into center of steak should register 145°F.) Transfer steaks to cutting board; keep warm.

4 To drippings in skillet, add shallots and cook over medium heat until browned and tender, 3 to 4 minutes. Add wine to skillet and heat to boiling over high heat. Boil 2 minutes.

5 To serve, thinly slice steaks and spoon wine sauce on top.

EACH SERVING: ABOUT 530 CALORIES | 30G PROTEIN | 2G CARBOHYDRATE | 40G TOTAL FAT (16G SATURATED) | 0G FIBER | 118MG CHOLESTEROL | 397MG SODIUM

STRIP STEAK WITH RED PEPPER VINAIGRETTE

A colorful, flavorful vinaigrette dresses up succulent grilled steak. Pair each serving with 1 cup sliced steamed zucchini tossed with olive oil, lemon juice, and fresh parsley—it's a sprightly side that adds just 5 grams of carbs to the meal.

ACTIVE TIME: 10 MINUTES · TOTAL TIME: 20 MINUTES

MAKES: 4 MAIN-DISH SERVINGS

1	LARGE GARLIC CLOVE	¼	CUP OLIVE OIL
¼	CUP LOOSELY PACKED FRESH PARSLEY LEAVES	½	SMALL RED PEPPER, CUT INTO ¼-INCH CUBES
1	TABLESPOON FRESH OREGANO LEAVES	1	PLUM TOMATO, SEEDED AND CHOPPED
½	CUP RED WINE VINEGAR	2	BONELESS BEEF TOP LOIN (STRIP) OR RIB-EYE STEAKS, ¾ INCH THICK (10 OUNCES EACH)
1	TEASPOON PAPRIKA		
1	TEASPOON CHILI POWDER	¼	TEASPOON COARSELY GROUND BLACK PEPPER
¾	TEASPOON SALT		

1   In blender, pulse garlic, parsley, and oregano until coarsely chopped. Add vinegar, paprika, chili powder, and ¼ teaspoon salt; blend until well combined. With blender running, add oil through hole in cover in slow, steady stream until mixture thickens. Transfer to small bowl; stir in red pepper and tomato. If not serving right away, cover and refrigerate up to 2 days. Makes about 1 cup vinaigrette.

2   Heat nonstick 10-inch skillet over medium heat until very hot. Sprinkle steaks with pepper and remaining ½ teaspoon salt. Place steaks in skillet; cook 3 to 5 minutes per side for medium-rare or to desired doneness. (Instant-read thermometer inserted horizontally into center of steak should register 145°F.) Serve with vinaigrette.

EACH SERVING STEAK WITH 2 TABLESPOONS VINAIGRETTE: ABOUT 295 CALORIES | 30G PROTEIN | 2G CARBOHYDRATE | 19G TOTAL FAT (6G SATURATED) | 0G FIBER | 82MG CHOLESTEROL | 440MG SODIUM 🟢 ☺ ♥

PEPPER-CRUSTED FILET MIGNON

Time to fire up the barbecue! The grilled sweet peppers are a nice foil to the pepper-studded steak. Toss some corn on the cob on the grill at the same time; you can enjoy half a cob slathered with butter for 16 grams carbs.

ACTIVE TIME: 15 MINUTES · TOTAL TIME: 35 MINUTES PLUS STANDING
MAKES: 4 MAIN-DISH SERVINGS

1   TABLESPOON WHOLE BLACK PEPPERCORNS

1   TEASPOON WHOLE FENNEL SEEDS

4   BEEF TENDERLOIN STEAKS (FILET MIGNON), 1 INCH THICK (4 OUNCES EACH)

3   PEPPERS (RED, YELLOW, AND/OR ORANGE)

1   TABLESPOON MINCED FRESH PARSLEY LEAVES

1   TEASPOON OLIVE OIL

¾   TEASPOON SALT

1   Prepare outdoor grill for direct grilling over medium-high heat.

2   Meanwhile, on cutting board, with rolling pin, crush peppercorns and fennel seeds. With hands, pat spice mixture around edges of steaks. Cover and refrigerate steaks up to 24 hours, until ready to cook.

3   Cut each pepper lengthwise in half; discard stems and seeds. With hand, flatten each pepper half.

4   Place peppers, skin side down, on hot grill rack. Cover and grill until skins are charred and blistered, 8 to 10 minutes. Transfer peppers to bowl; cover with plate and let steam at room temperature about 15 minutes, until cool enough to handle. Adjust grill temperature to medium.

5   Remove peppers from bowl. Peel off skins and discard. Cut peppers lengthwise into ¼-inch-wide strips. Return to same bowl and toss with parsley, oil, and ¼ teaspoon salt.

6   Sprinkle steaks with remaining ½ teaspoon salt. Place on hot grill rack. Cover and grill 4 to 5 minutes per side for medium-rare or to desired doneness. (Instant-read thermometer inserted horizontally into center of steak should register 145°F.) Serve steaks topped with grilled peppers.

EACH SERVING: ABOUT 230 CALORIES | 26G PROTEIN | 9G CARBOHYDRATE | 10G TOTAL FAT (3G SATURATED) | 2G FIBER | 71MG CHOLESTEROL | 495MG SODIUM ☺

IS THAT STEAK DONE YET?

You've got three options when it comes to determining the done-ness of a steak.

1. Using an instant-read meat thermometer, check the steak's internal temperature. Insert the thermometer horizontally into the center of the steak, taking care to avoid any bone or gristle to ensure an accurate reading of the meat's temperature.

2. Cut a small slit in the meat near the bone or near the center of a boneless steak. Rare steak will be bright red in the center and pinkish toward the surface; medium-rare, very pink in the center and slightly brown toward the surface; medium, light pink in the center with a brown outer portion; and well-done, uniformly brown throughout. (Unlike hamburgers, steak can safely be eaten rare or medium-rare.)

3. To test doneness without cutting, try the chef's method: Compare the feel of the meat, without cutting it, in the top center of the steak to the skin between the thumb and index finger when your hand is relaxed (hanging loosely), lightly fisted, and tightly clenched. A rare steak feels soft and spongy and offers very little resistance when pressed, similar to a relaxed hand. A medium-rare steak is springy to the touch, as on a loosely fisted hand. Medium steak feels firm, with minimal give, like a tight fist.

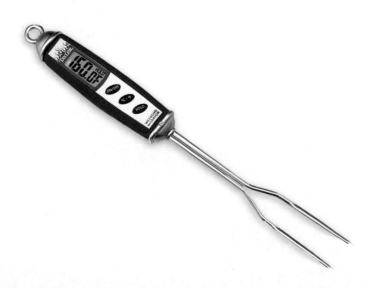

FILET MIGNON WITH HORSERADISH SALSA

Juicy steaks taste even better with our flavor-packed salsa. Serve with charbroiled portobellos on the side; one cup sliced mushrooms adds just 5 grams of carbs to the meal.

ACTIVE TIME: 15 MINUTES · TOTAL TIME: 25 MINUTES
MAKES: 4 MAIN-DISH SERVINGS

HORSERADISH SALSA

- 1 POUND RIPE TOMATOES, CUT INTO ½-INCH PIECES
- 1 CUP LOOSELY PACKED FRESH PARSLEY LEAVES, CHOPPED
- ½ SMALL RED ONION, MINCED
- 2 TABLESPOONS BOTTLED WHITE HORSERADISH
- 1 TABLESPOON BALSAMIC VINEGAR
- 1 TABLESPOON OLIVE OIL
- ½ TEASPOON SALT

FILET MIGNON

- 1 TEASPOON CRACKED BLACK PEPPER
- 1 TEASPOON OLIVE OIL
- ½ TEASPOON SALT
- ¼ TEASPOON DRIED THYME
- 1 GARLIC CLOVE, CRUSHED WITH GARLIC PRESS
- 4 BEEF TENDERLOIN STEAKS (FILET MIGNON), 1 INCH THICK (6 OUNCES EACH)

1 Prepare salsa: In medium bowl, place tomatoes, parsley, onion, horseradish, vinegar, oil, and salt; toss to combine. Makes about 2 cups. Cover and refrigerate up to 2 hours.

2 Prepare outdoor grill for direct grilling over medium heat, or lightly spray a ridged grill pan with nonstick cooking spray, then place over medium heat until hot.

3 In cup, mix pepper, oil, salt, thyme, and garlic. Rub mixture all over steaks.

4 Place steaks on hot grill rack or pan and cook, turning over once, 10 to 12 minutes for medium-rare or to desired doneness. (Instant-read thermometer inserted horizontally into center of steak should register 145°F.) Serve steaks with salsa.

EACH SERVING STEAK WITH ½ CUP SALSA: ABOUT 330 CALORIES | 39G PROTEIN | 9G CARBOHYDRATE | 15G TOTAL FAT (4G SATURATED) | 89MG CHOLESTEROL | 710MG SODIUM ♥ ☺

LEMONY VEAL AND BABY ARTICHOKES

Tiny artichokes pair up perfectly with tender veal cutlets in a brothy sauce that's lightly flecked with fresh tarragon and shallots. Once trimmed, the baby artichokes are completely edible because the fibrous chokes haven't developed yet.

ACTIVE TIME: 30 MINUTES · TOTAL TIME: 55 MINUTES
MAKES: 4 MAIN-DISH SERVINGS

---

8   BABY ARTICHOKES
    (12 OUNCES; SEE TIP)

1   POUND VEAL CUTLETS, EACH CUT IN
    HALF IF LARGE

1   LEMON

2   TEASPOONS OLIVE OIL

½   TEASPOON SALT

¼   TEASPOON GROUND BLACK PEPPER

2   SHALLOTS, THINLY SLICED

½   CUP WATER

1   CUP CHICKEN BROTH

1   TABLESPOON ALL-PURPOSE FLOUR

1   TEASPOON MINCED FRESH
    TARRAGON LEAVES

1   Trim artichokes: Bend back outer all-green leaves and snap off at base until remaining leaves are green on top and yellow at bottom. Cut stems off, level with bottom of artichokes. Cut off and discard top half of each artichoke.

2   In nonstick 12-inch skillet, heat ½ *inch salted water* to boiling over medium-high heat. Add artichokes; reduce heat to medium-low and cook, covered, until artichokes are fork-tender, 12 minutes. Drain in colander; cool until easy to handle. Cut each baby artichoke lengthwise into quarters. Do not discard center portion.

3   Meanwhile, if necessary, with meat mallet, pound veal cutlets to even ⅛-inch thickness. From lemon, grate 2 teaspoons peel and squeeze 1 table-spoon juice.

4   In same skillet, heat 1 teaspoon oil over medium heat until hot but not smoking. Add half of cutlets; sprinkle with ¼ teaspoon salt and ⅛ teaspoon pepper and cook until cutlets just lose pink color throughout, 2 to 3 min-utes, turning over once. Transfer cutlets to platter and keep warm. Repeat with remaining cutlets, 1 teaspoon oil, ¼ teaspoon salt, and ⅛ teaspoon pepper (reduce heat to medium if cutlets brown too quickly).

5   To same skillet, add shallots and water and cook over medium heat 1 minute. In cup, mix broth and flour. Increase heat to medium-high; add broth mixture and lemon peel and boil until slightly thickened, 1 minute. Add artichokes, tarragon, and lemon juice; cook 1 minute to heat through, stirring gently.

6   To serve, spoon artichokes with sauce over veal on platter.

TIP   If you can't find baby artichokes, you can use the regular-sized ones. Look for two medium artichokes, about 4 ounces each. To trim them, use a serrated knife and cut 1 inch straight across the top of each artichoke. Cut off the stems; pull the dark outer leaves off the bottoms. With kitchen shears, trim thorny tips from the remaining leaves. Cut the artichokes lengthwise into sixths. Scrape out and discard the chokes, removing the centermost petals along with fuzzy center portions. Rinse the artichokes well and proceed with step 2, but do not cut the pieces into quarters.

EACH SERVING: ABOUT 180 CALORIES | 27G PROTEIN | 7G CARBOHYDRATE | 5G TOTAL FAT (1G SATURATED) | 2G FIBER | 89MG CHOLESTEROL | 795MG SODIUM ☺

THAI BEEF SALAD

This hearty salad makes a great one-dish meal. Steak is marinated in an Asian-style dressing before it's grilled and served on top of a watercress salad tossed with mint, cilantro, radishes, and red onion.

ACTIVE TIME: 30 MINUTES · TOTAL TIME: 40 MINUTES PLUS MARINATING
MAKES: 4 MAIN-DISH SERVINGS

- 2 TABLESPOONS SUGAR-FREE ASIAN FISH SAUCE (SEE TIP, PAGE 21)
- ZERO-CALORIE SWEETENER (1 TABLESPOON EQUIVALENT)
- 1 BEEF TOP ROUND STEAK, ¾ INCH THICK (1 POUND)
- 2 LIMES
- 3 TABLESPOONS VEGETABLE OIL
- ¼ TEASPOON CRUSHED RED PEPPER
- ¼ TEASPOON COARSELY GROUND BLACK PEPPER
- 2 BUNCHES WATERCRESS, TOUGH STEMS DISCARDED
- 1 CUP LOOSELY PACKED FRESH MINT LEAVES
- 1 CUP LOOSELY PACKED FRESH CILANTRO LEAVES
- 1 BUNCH RADISHES, EACH CUT IN HALF AND THINLY SLICED
- ½ SMALL RED ONION, THINLY SLICED

1 In 8-inch or 9-inch square glass baking dish, stir 1 tablespoon fish sauce and half of sweetener. Add steak, turning to coat; marinate 15 minutes at room temperature or 1 hour in refrigerator, turning occasionally.

2 Prepare outdoor grill for direct grilling over medium heat.

3 Meanwhile, from limes, with vegetable peeler, remove peel in 2" by ¾" strips. With sharp knife, cut enough peel crosswise into matchstick-thin strips to equal 1 tablespoon. Squeeze limes to equal 3 tablespoons juice. In small bowl, whisk lime juice, oil, crushed red pepper, black pepper, and the remaining 1 tablespoon fish sauce and half of sweetener until blended.

4 In large bowl, toss watercress, mint, cilantro, radishes, onion, and lime peel; cover and refrigerate until ready to serve.

5 Place steak on hot grill rack. Cover grill and cook steak 10 to 15 minutes for medium-rare or to desired doneness, turning over once. (Instant-read thermometer inserted horizontally into center of steak should register 145°F.) Transfer steak to cutting board; let stand 10 minutes to set juices for easier slicing. Cut steak diagonally into thin strips.

6 Add steak and dressing to watercress mixture and toss until well coated.

EACH SERVING: ABOUT 310 CALORIES | 28G PROTEIN | 7G CARBOHYDRATE | 23G TOTAL FAT (4G SATURATED) | 2G FIBER | 73MG CHOLESTEROL | 295MG SODIUM ☺ ♥

GRILLED STEAK CAESAR SALAD

This classic salad becomes a luscious meal when it's tossed with slices of juicy grilled steak. Prepare the steak indoors in a grill pan for ease.

ACTIVE TIME: 25 MINUTES · TOTAL TIME: 35 MINUTES PLUS STANDING
MAKES: 4 MAIN-DISH SERVINGS

- ½ LOAF FRENCH BREAD (4 OUNCES), CUT INTO ¾-INCH CUBES (3 CUPS)
- 5 TABLESPOONS OLIVE OIL
- 4 ANCHOVY FILLETS, DRAINED
- 1 GARLIC CLOVE, CRUSHED WITH GARLIC PRESS
- ¼ CUP GRATED PARMESAN CHEESE
- 3 TABLESPOONS FRESH LEMON JUICE
- 1 TEASPOON WORCESTERSHIRE SAUCE
- ½ TEASPOON DRY MUSTARD
- ½ TEASPOON SALT
- ¼ TEASPOON COARSELY GROUND BLACK PEPPER
- 2 BONELESS BEEF TOP LOIN (SHELL) STEAKS, 1 INCH THICK (8 OUNCES EACH)
- 2 HEADS ROMAINE LETTUCE, CUT CROSSWISE INTO ½-INCH SLICES (10 CUPS)

1   Preheat oven to 350°F. In 15½" by 10½" jelly-roll pan, toss bread cubes with 1 tablespoon oil. Toast bread in oven, stirring occasionally, until golden brown, 15 to 20 minutes. Cool croutons in pan on wire rack.

2   Meanwhile, in medium bowl, mash anchovies with garlic to form paste. With wire whisk, mix in Parmesan, lemon juice, Worcestershire, mustard, ¼ teaspoon salt, and ⅛ teaspoon pepper. Gradually whisk in remaining ¼ cup oil until well blended. Set dressing aside.

3   Preheat ridged grill pan over medium heat until very hot. Place steaks in pan; sprinkle with remaining ¼ teaspoon salt and ⅛ teaspoon pepper. Cook steaks 5 to 6 minutes per side for medium-rare or to desired doneness. (Instant-read thermometer inserted horizontally into center of steak should register 145°F.) Transfer steaks to cutting board; let stand 10 minutes to set juices for easier slicing.

4   To serve, thinly slice steaks diagonally against grain. In large serving bowl, toss romaine with steak slices, croutons, and dressing.

EACH SERVING: ABOUT 465 CALORIES | 32G PROTEIN | 20G CARBOHYDRATE | 29G TOTAL FAT (7G SATURATED) | 3G FIBER | 73MG CHOLESTEROL | 785MG SODIUM

KOREAN-STYLE SIRLOIN

Let the steak soak up the gingery Asian-style marinade before you grill it, then serve even more sauce on the side for terrific flavor. Steamed broccoli with a spritz of lemon and a touch of butter would make an ideal accompaniment that adds just 5 grams of carbs per serving.

ACTIVE TIME: 10 MINUTES · TOTAL TIME: 25 MINUTES PLUS MARINATING
MAKES: 4 MAIN-DISH SERVINGS

½ CUP REDUCED-SODIUM SOY SAUCE

2 TABLESPOONS GRATED, PEELED FRESH GINGER

ZERO-CALORIE SWEETENER (1 TABLESPOON EQUIVALENT)

1 TABLESPOON ASIAN SESAME OIL

¼ TEASPOON CAYENNE (GROUND RED) PEPPER

3 GARLIC CLOVES, FINELY CHOPPED

1 BONELESS BEEF TOP SIRLOIN OR TOP ROUND STEAK, 1 INCH THICK (1¼ POUNDS)

2 TABLESPOONS WATER

CHOPPED GREEN ONIONS FOR GARNISH

1   In small bowl, stir together soy sauce, ginger, sweetener, sesame oil, cayenne, and garlic.

2   Pour marinade into large resealable plastic bag; add steak, turning to coat. Seal bag, pressing out excess air. Place bag on plate; refrigerate 1 hour or up to 4 hours, turning bag over several times.

3   Heat ridged grill pan over medium-high heat until very hot. Remove steak from bag; pour marinade into 1-quart saucepan and reserve. Pat steak dry with paper towels. Cook steak 6 to 8 minutes per side for medium-rare or to desired doneness. (Instant-read thermometer inserted horizontally into steak should register 145°F.)

4   Transfer steak to cutting board; let stand 10 minutes to set juices for easier slicing. Meanwhile, add water to marinade in saucepan; heat to boiling over high heat. Boil 2 minutes.

5   To serve, thinly slice steak diagonally against grain. Transfer steak to platter and garnish with green onions. Serve with cooked marinade on the side.

EACH SERVING: ABOUT 365 CALORIES | 35G PROTEIN | 7G CARBOHYDRATE | 21G TOTAL FAT (8G SATURATED) | 0G FIBER | 102MG CHOLESTEROL | 1,160MG SODIUM

CHILE STEAK WITH AVOCADO-TOMATO SALAD

Thinly cut slices of spicy grilled skirt steak are topped with a fresh, bright avocado and tomato salad.

ACTIVE TIME: 15 MINUTES · **TOTAL TIME:** 20 MINUTES
MAKES: 4 MAIN-DISH SERVINGS

CHILE STEAK

- 2 CHIPOTLE CHILES IN ADOBO (SEE TIP), FINELY CHOPPED
- 2 GARLIC CLOVES, CRUSHED WITH GARLIC PRESS
- 2 TEASPOONS FRESH LIME JUICE
- 1 TEASPOON DRIED OREGANO, CRUSHED
- ¾ TEASPOON SALT
- ¼ TEASPOON COARSELY GROUND PEPPER
- 1 BEEF SKIRT STEAK (1¼ POUNDS)

AVOCADO-TOMATO SALAD

- 1 PINT RED OR YELLOW CHERRY TOMATOES, CUT IN HALF
- 1 RIPE AVOCADO, PITTED, PEELED, AND CUT INTO ¾-INCH CHUNKS
- 1 TABLESPOON COARSELY CHOPPED FRESH CILANTRO LEAVES
- 2 TEASPOONS FRESH LIME JUICE
- ⅛ TEASPOON SALT

1   Prepare steak: In cup, mix chipotles, garlic, and lime juice; set aside. In another cup, mix oregano, salt, and pepper; rub all over steak.

2   Heat ridged grill pan over medium-high heat until very hot. Place steak in pan; brush top with half of chipotle mixture and cook 2 minutes. Turn steak over; brush with remaining chipotle mixture and cook 2 to 3 minutes longer for medium-rare or to desired doneness. (Instant-read thermometer inserted horizontally into center of steak should register 145°F.) Turn steak over again; cook 30 seconds. Transfer to cutting board; keep warm.

3   Meanwhile, prepare salad: In bowl, mix tomatoes, avocado, cilantro, lime juice, and salt. Makes about 3 cups.

4   Thinly slice steak; serve with avocado salad.

TIP   Canned chipotle chiles are smoked jalapeño chiles packed in a thick, vinegary sauce called *adobo*. Look for them in Latin-American markets and in the international section of many supermarkets.

EACH SERVING STEAK WITH ¾ CUP SALAD: ABOUT 350 CALORIES | 36G PROTEIN | 9G CARBOHYDRATE | 19G TOTAL FAT (5G SATURATED) | 3G FIBER | 108MG CHOLESTEROL | 947MG SODIUM ✔ ☺

LONDON BROIL WITH GARLIC AND HERBS

Round steak, not the most tender of cuts, benefits from a quick marinade of vinegar, garlic, and oregano. For a tasty side dish, grill tomato halves brushed with olive oil and sprinkled with Parmesan alongside the steak. Two halves adds just 5 grams of carbs to the meal.

ACTIVE TIME: 10 MINUTES · TOTAL TIME: 25 MINUTES PLUS MARINATING AND STANDING
MAKES: 6 MAIN-DISH SERVINGS

2	TABLESPOONS RED WINE VINEGAR	¾	TEASPOON SALT
1	TABLESPOON OLIVE OIL	½	TEASPOON GROUND BLACK PEPPER
2	GARLIC CLOVES, CRUSHED WITH GARLIC PRESS	1	BEEF TOP ROUND STEAK, 1 INCH THICK (1½ POUNDS)
¾	TEASPOON DRIED OREGANO		

1 Prepare outdoor grill for direct grilling over medium heat. In large resealable plastic bag, mix vinegar, oil, garlic, oregano, salt, and pepper. Add steak, turning to coat. Seal bag, pressing out excess air. Place bag on plate and marinate 15 minutes at room temperature.

2 Remove steak from marinade; discard marinade. Place steak on hot grill rack. Grill 7 to 8 minutes per side for medium-rare or to desired doneness. (Instant-read thermometer inserted horizontally into center of steak should register 145°F.)

3 Transfer steak to platter. Let stand 10 minutes to set juices for easier slicing. To serve, thinly slice steak across the grain.

EACH SERVING: ABOUT 200 CALORIES | 26G PROTEIN | 1G CARBOHYDRATE | 10G TOTAL FAT (3G SATURATED) | 0G FIBER | 72MG CHOLESTEROL | 340MG SODIUM ☺ ♥

SKIRT STEAK WITH CHIMICHURRI SAUCE

This fresh and flavorful garlic and herb sauce hails from Argentina, where it's paired with various grilled meats. Wrap the steak in Romaine leaves to add a bit of crunch.

ACTIVE TIME: 15 MINUTES · TOTAL TIME: 25 MINUTES PLUS STANDING
MAKES: 4 MAIN-DISH SERVINGS

CHIMICHURRI SAUCE

- 1 GARLIC CLOVE, CRUSHED WITH GARLIC PRESS
- ¼ TEASPOON SALT
- 1 CUP LOOSELY PACKED FRESH ITALIAN PARSLEY LEAVES, CHOPPED
- 1 CUP LOOSELY PACKED FRESH CILANTRO LEAVES, CHOPPED
- 2 TABLESPOONS OLIVE OIL
- 1 TABLESPOON RED WINE VINEGAR
- ¼ TEASPOON CRUSHED RED PEPPER

STEAK

- 1 BEEF SKIRT STEAK OR FLANK STEAK (1¼ POUNDS)
- ¼ TEASPOON SALT
- ⅛ TEASPOON COARSELY GROUND BLACK PEPPER

1 Prepare chimichurri sauce: In small bowl, stir together garlic, salt, parsley, cilantro, oil, vinegar, and crushed red pepper until mixed. (Alternatively, pulse ingredients in mini food processor or blender just until mixed.) Makes about ¼ cup. Sauce can be refrigerated up to 2 days; bring it to room temperature before serving.

2 Prepare outdoor grill for direct grilling over medium heat.

3 Sprinkle steak with salt and pepper; place on hot grill rack. Cover and grill 3 minutes per side for medium-rare or to desired doneness. (Instant-read thermometer inserted horizontally into center should register 145°F.)

4 Transfer steak to cutting board; let stand 10 minutes to set juices for easier slicing. Thinly slice steak crosswise against the grain. Serve with chimichurri sauce.

EACH SERVING STEAK WITH 1 TABLESPOON SAUCE: ABOUT 300 CALORIES | 40G PROTEIN 1G CARBOHYDRATE | 14G TOTAL FAT (5G SATURATED) | 1G FIBER | 121MG CHOLESTEROL 380MG SODIUM ☺ ♥

POT ROAST WITH RED WINE SAUCE

Classic French flavors like thyme, pearl onions, and red wine season this easy slow-cooker meal. Use the leftovers to make the Pot Roast Chili recipe opposite, pictured on page 6.

ACTIVE TIME: 20 MINUTES · SLOW-COOK TIME: 10 HOURS
MAKES: 6 MAIN-DISH SERVINGS

1	BONELESS BEEF CHUCK ROAST (4½ POUNDS), TIED
¼	TEASPOON SALT
¼	TEASPOON GROUND BLACK PEPPER
1	TEASPOON VEGETABLE OIL
1	POUND CARROTS
1	POUND FROZEN PEARL ONIONS
3	CLOVES GARLIC, PRESSED WITH GARLIC PRESS
½	TEASPOON DRIED THYME
1	CUP DRY RED WINE
1	CAN (28 OUNCES) NO-SALT-ADDED TOMATOES, DICED AND DRAINED
1	BAY LEAF
	FRESH FLAT-LEAF PARSLEY LEAVES, CHOPPED, FOR GARNISH

1   With paper towels, pat beef dry; season with salt and pepper.

2   In 12-inch skillet, heat oil on medium-high. Add beef and cook 10 to 13 minutes, turning to brown all sides. Transfer to 6-quart slow-cooker bowl.

3   While beef browns, peel carrots and cut into 2-inch chunks. Transfer to slow-cooker bowl.

4   To same skillet, add onions, garlic, and thyme. Cook 2 minutes or until golden, stirring often. Add wine; cook 3 minutes, stirring and scraping up browned bits. Transfer to slow-cooker bowl, along with tomatoes and bay leaf; cover with lid and cook on Low 10 hours.

5   Transfer beef to cutting board; discard strings. Cut off one-third of beef; transfer to container along with one-third of vegetables. Refrigerate up to 3 days. Transfer remaining vegetables to serving platter; discard bay leaf.

6   Transfer cooking liquid from slow-cooker bowl to 8-cup liquid measuring cup; discard fat. Pour one-third of liquid into container; refrigerate up to 3 days.

7   Slice meat across grain and arrange on serving platter with vegetables. Pour remaining cooking liquid over all. Garnish with parsley.

EACH SERVING: ABOUT 515 CALORIES | 47G PROTEIN | 11G CARBOHYDRATE | 30G TOTAL FAT (12G SATURATED) | 3G FIBER | 181MG CHOLESTEROL | 205MG SODIUM

POT ROAST CHILI

The chuck roast in red wine sauce kick-starts beef chili's full-bodied flavor. After serving most of the meat for the first evening's meal, quick-cook the rest with cumin and beans for this speedy second-day supper.

ACTIVE TIME: 5 MINUTES · TOTAL TIME: 20 MINUTES

MAKES: 6 MAIN-DISH SERVINGS.

Chop reserved **beef and vegetables.** In 5-quart saucepot, heat **1 teaspoon vegetable oil** on medium heat. Add **2 garlic cloves,** pressed; **1 tablespoon plus 1 teaspoon ground cumin;** and **1 teaspoon chili powder.** Cook 2 minutes, stirring. Stir in **2 cans (15 ounces each) no-salt-added black beans,** drained and rinsed; chopped beef and vegetables; reserved **cooking liquid;** and ¼ teaspoon salt. Heat to boiling, then reduce heat to simmer 10 minutes, stirring occasionally. Serve with **chopped fresh cilantro, sour cream,** and **lime wedges.**

EACH SERVING: ABOUT 380 CALORIES | 31G PROTEIN | 26G CARBOHYDRATE | 16G TOTAL FAT (6G SATURATED) | 9G FIBER | 91MG CHOLESTEROL | 225MG SODIUM ❤ ☺

BEEF BURGUNDY

A hearty beef and mushroom stew flavored with dry red wine makes for a perfect midwinter supper.

ACTIVE TIME: 1 HOUR · TOTAL TIME: 2 HOURS 30 MINUTES
MAKES: 10 MAIN-DISH SERVINGS

2 SLICES BACON, CUT INTO ½-INCH PIECES

3 POUNDS BONELESS BEEF CHUCK, TRIMMED AND CUT INTO 1½-INCH CUBES

5 CARROTS, EACH PEELED AND CUT INTO ½-INCH PIECES

3 GARLIC CLOVES, CRUSHED WITH SIDE OF CHEF'S KNIFE

1 LARGE ONION (12 OUNCES), CUT INTO 1-INCH PIECES

2 TABLESPOONS ALL-PURPOSE FLOUR

2 TABLESPOONS TOMATO PASTE

1 TEASPOON SALT

½ TEASPOON COARSELY GROUND BLACK PEPPER

2 CUPS DRY RED WINE

4 SPRIGS FRESH THYME

1 PACKAGE (12 OUNCES) MUSHROOMS, EACH TRIMMED AND CUT INTO QUARTERS, OR HALVES IF SMALL

½ CUP LOOSELY PACKED FRESH PARSLEY LEAVES, CHOPPED

1   In 5- to 6-quart Dutch oven, cook bacon over medium heat until browned. With slotted spoon, transfer to medium bowl.

2   Pat beef dry with paper towels. Add beef, in three batches, to bacon drippings and cook over medium-high heat until well browned on all sides, about 5 minutes per batch. With slotted spoon, transfer beef to bowl with bacon.

3   Preheat oven to 325°F. To drippings in Dutch oven, add carrots, garlic, and onion and cook, stirring occasionally, until vegetables are browned and tender, about 10 minutes. Stir in flour, tomato paste, salt, and pepper; cook, stirring, 2 minutes. Add wine and heat to boiling, stirring until browned bits are loosened from bottom of Dutch oven.

4   Return meat, meat juices, and bacon to Dutch oven. Add thyme and mushrooms; heat to boiling. Cover Dutch oven and bake until meat is fork-tender, 1 hour 30 minutes to 2 hours, stirring once. Skim and discard fat from liquid; discard thyme sprigs. Sprinkle with parsley to serve.

EACH SERVING: ABOUT 295 CALORIES | 36G PROTEIN | 9G CARBOHYDRATE | 11G TOTAL FAT (4G SATURATED) | 2G FIBER | 89MG CHOLESTEROL | 375MG SODIUM ☺ ♥ ▄

BRACIOLE WITH GRAPE TOMATOES

This Italian stuffed and rolled beef specialty is traditionally simmered slowly in tomato sauce. We offer a quicker method: roasting the beef at high heat and pairing it with tiny sweet grape tomatoes. Serve with a side of broccoli rabe sautéed with garlic and sprinkled with Parmesan cheese; one serving costs you just 3 grams of carbs. For photo, see page 42.

ACTIVE TIME: 15 MINUTES · TOTAL TIME: 40 MINUTES PLUS STANDING
MAKES: 8 MAIN-DISH SERVINGS

½ CUP ITALIAN-STYLE BREAD CRUMBS

1 GARLIC CLOVE, CRUSHED WITH GARLIC PRESS

¼ CUP FINELY GRATED PECORINO ROMANO CHEESE

½ CUP PACKED FRESH FLAT-LEAF PARSLEY LEAVES, FINELY CHOPPED

4 TEASPOONS OLIVE OIL

½ TEASPOON GROUND BLACK PEPPER

1 BEEF FLANK STEAK (1¾ TO 2 POUNDS)

¼ TEASPOON SALT

2 PINTS GRAPE TOMATOES

1   Preheat oven to 475°F. In small bowl, combine bread crumbs, garlic, Pecorino, parsley, 1 tablespoon oil, and ¼ teaspoon pepper.

2   On large sheet of waxed paper, with flat side of meat mallet or heavy skillet, pound steak to even ½-inch thickness. Spread crumb mixture over steak in even layer; press into meat. Starting at one long side, roll steak into cylinder (about 3 inches in diameter) to enclose filling completely. (Some bread crumbs may spill out.) With butcher's twine or kitchen string, tie roll tightly at 1-inch intervals. Place roll in center of 18" by 12" jelly-roll pan. Rub salt and remaining 1 teaspoon oil and ¼ teaspoon pepper all over steak. Scatter tomatoes around steak.

3   Roast 25 to 27 minutes or until temperature on instant-read thermometer, inserted into thickest part of roll, registers 135°F. Let steak stand in pan 10 minutes to set juices for easier slicing. Remove and discard twine; cut roll crosswise into ½-inch-thick slices. Transfer meat and tomatoes with their juices to serving platter.

EACH SERVING: ABOUT 225 CALORIES | 22G PROTEIN | 10G CARBOHYDRATE | 14G TOTAL FAT (5G SATURATED) | 1G FIBER | 54MG CHOLESTEROL | 290MG SODIUM ☺ ♥ 🍽

PORK & LAMB

The flavor and aroma of pork tenderloin, chops, ham, and ribs can't be beat. We offer succulent recipes for them all—savor Mushroom Glazed Pork Chops, Chili-Rubbed Ham with Peach Salsa, or Kansas City Ribs. Or, for something different, try lamb: Our pan-seared Middle Eastern Lamb Steaks are paired with a tangy tomato relish.

KEY TO ICONS

◐ 30 minutes or less   ☺ Low calorie   ♥ Heart healthy   ▬ Make ahead   ⬛ Slow cooker

Pork Medallions with Asparagus Salad (page 75)

SPICY GROUND LAMB AND VEGGIE KABOBS

These Middle Eastern–style kabobs are served with a yogurt sauce flavored with lemon juice and three herbs. Serve it with a salad of chopped tomatoes and cucumbers tossed with olive oil and lemon juice.

ACTIVE TIME: 35 MINUTES · **TOTAL TIME:** 45 MINUTES
MAKES: 4 MAIN-DISH SERVINGS

HERBED YOGURT SAUCE

1   CUP PLAIN LOW-FAT YOGURT

2   TABLESPOONS MINCED FRESH DILL

2   TABLESPOONS MINCED FRESH CILANTRO

1   TABLESPOON MINCED FRESH OREGANO LEAVES (OPTIONAL)

1   TABLESPOON FRESH LEMON JUICE

⅛   TEASPOON SALT

LAMB AND VEGETABLE KABOBS

1   POUND GROUND LAMB

2   GREEN ONIONS, MINCED

2   GARLIC CLOVES, CRUSHED WITH GARLIC PRESS

1   JALAPEÑO CHILE, SEEDED AND MINCED

2   TABLESPOONS MINCED FRESH CILANTRO

2   TEASPOONS GRATED, PEELED FRESH GINGER

½   TEASPOON GROUND CORIANDER

½   TEASPOON GROUND CUMIN

1¼ TEASPOONS SALT

⅜   TEASPOON GROUND BLACK PEPPER

1   MEDIUM JAPANESE EGGPLANT (5 OUNCES; SEE TIP)

1   RED ONION

1   GREEN OR RED PEPPER

1   LARGE PORTOBELLO MUSHROOM (6 OUNCES), STEM DISCARDED

1   TABLESPOON OLIVE OIL

4   LONG ALL-METAL SKEWERS (SEE BOX, PAGE 29)

1 Prepare sauce: In small serving bowl, stir yogurt with dill, cilantro, oregano (if using), lemon juice, and salt. Cover and refrigerate until ready to serve. Makes about 1 cup.

2 Preheat broiler and set rack as close to heating element as possible.

3 Prepare kabobs: In medium bowl, combine lamb, green onions, garlic, jalapeño, cilantro, ginger, coriander, cumin, ¾ teaspoon salt, and ¼ teaspoon black pepper just until blended but not overmixed; set aside. Cut eggplant, red onion, green pepper, and mushroom into 8 pieces each. Toss vegetables with oil, remaining ½ teaspoon salt, and ⅛ teaspoon black pepper.

4 On each skewer, thread 2 pieces of each vegetable. With hands, shape one-fourth of lamb mixture around remaining length of each skewer. Place skewers on rack in broiling pan. Broil skewers until lamb is cooked through and vegetables are lightly browned and tender, 10 minutes, turning once. Serve lamb and vegetables with yogurt sauce.

TIP Ranging in color from solid purple to striated to white, Japanese eggplants are very narrow and straight in shape. Their flesh is tender and slightly sweet.

EACH KABOB WITH ¼ CUP SAUCE: ABOUT 365 CALORIES | 28G PROTEIN | 16G CARBOHY-DRATE | 20G TOTAL FAT (7G SATURATED) | 4G FIBER | 87MG CHOLESTEROL | 925MG SODIUM ☺

ORANGE PORK AND ASPARAGUS STIR-FRY

Slices of lean pork tenderloin are quickly cooked with fresh asparagus and juicy orange pieces to create a light, flavorful meal.

ACTIVE TIME: 20 MINUTES · **TOTAL TIME:** 25 MINUTES
MAKES: 4 MAIN-DISH SERVINGS

- 2 NAVEL ORANGES
- 1 TEASPOON OLIVE OIL
- 1 PORK TENDERLOIN (12 OUNCES), TRIMMED, THINLY SLICED DIAGONALLY
- ¾ TEASPOON SALT
- ¼ TEASPOON GROUND BLACK PEPPER

- 1½ POUNDS THIN ASPARAGUS, TRIMMED, EACH STALK CUT IN HALF
- 1 GARLIC CLOVE, CRUSHED WITH GARLIC PRESS
- ¼ CUP WATER

1 From 1 orange, grate 1 teaspoon peel and squeeze ¼ cup juice. Cut off peel and white pith from remaining orange. Cut orange into ¼-inch slices; cut each slice into quarters.

2 In nonstick 12-inch skillet, heat ½ teaspoon oil on medium until hot but not smoking. Add half of pork and sprinkle with ¼ teaspoon salt and ⅛ teaspoon pepper. Cook, stirring frequently, until pork just loses pink color, 2 to 3 minutes. Transfer pork to plate. Repeat with remaining ½ teaspoon oil, remaining half of pork, ¼ teaspoon salt, and remaining ⅛ teaspoon pepper. Transfer pork to same plate.

3 To same skillet, add asparagus, garlic, orange peel, water, and remaining ¼ teaspoon salt; cover and cook, stirring occasionally, until asparagus is tender-crisp, 2 to 3 minutes. Return pork to skillet. Add orange juice and orange pieces; heat through, stirring often.

EACH SERVING: ABOUT 165 CALORIES | 24G PROTEIN | 8G CARBOHYDRATE | 4G TOTAL FAT (1G SATURATED) | 2G FIBER | 50MG CHOLESTEROL | 495MG SODIUM ♥ ☺

CURRIED PORK AND APPLES

A simple skillet dinner: Tender slices of pork and tart apples are flavored with curry, then tossed with baby carrots. Serve with 4 cups shredded cabbage sautéed in olive oil and garnished with a splash of apple cider vinegar and 1 tablespoon toasted chopped pecans. Net carbs for the meal: 20.

ACTIVE TIME: 5 MINUTES · **TOTAL TIME:** 15 MINUTES

MAKES: 4 MAIN-DISH SERVINGS

1 BAG (16 OUNCES) PEELED BABY CARROTS

¼ CUP WATER

1 TABLESPOON OLIVE OIL

1 GALA OR GOLDEN DELICIOUS APPLE, UNPEELED, CORED, AND CUT INTO ½-INCH CUBES

2 TEASPOONS CURRY POWDER

1 GARLIC CLOVE, CRUSHED WITH GARLIC PRESS

1 PORK TENDERLOIN (1 POUND), TRIMMED AND CUT INTO ¾-INCH-THICK SLICES

½ TEASPOON SALT

¼ CUP APPLE CIDER OR APPLE JUICE

1 Place carrots in covered microwavable dish with water. Cook in microwave oven on High until carrots are tender, about 6 minutes.

2 Meanwhile, in nonstick 12-inch skillet, heat oil over medium heat. Add apple, curry powder, and garlic; cook, stirring, 1 minute.

3 Add pork and salt, and cook until pork is still slightly pink in center, 6 to 8 minutes. (An instant-read thermometer inserted horizontally into pork slices should register 145°F.) Add cider and cooked carrots with any liquid, and heat to boiling; cook 1 minute.

EACH SERVING: ABOUT 250 CALORIES | 25G PROTEIN | 17G CARBOHYDRATE | 9G TOTAL FAT (2G SATURATED) | 3G FIBER | 71MG CHOLESTEROL | 390MG SODIUM 💛 ☺ 🖤

PORK MEDALLIONS WITH ASPARAGUS SALAD

Herbed tenderloin is served atop a fiber-rich salad of crunchy carrots, asparagus, and greens. For photo, see page 68.

ACTIVE TIME: 20 MINUTES · **TOTAL TIME:** 40 MINUTES

MAKES: 4 MAIN-DISH SERVINGS

½ CUP PACKED FRESH FLAT-LEAF PARSLEY LEAVES	1 TEASPOON PLUS 1 TABLESPOON EXTRA-VIRGIN OLIVE OIL
1 TABLESPOON FRESH ROSEMARY, FINELY CHOPPED	1 BUNCH RADISHES, TRIMMED AND CUT INTO THIN WEDGES
1 PORK TENDERLOIN (12 OUNCES)	1 GREEN ONION, THINLY SLICED
2 LARGE CARROTS	1 PACKAGE (5 OUNCES) BABY GREENS AND HERBS MIX
1 POUND ASPARAGUS, ENDS TRIMMED	
¼ TEASPOON SALT	¼ CUP BALSAMIC VINEGAR
¼ TEASPOON FRESHLY GROUND BLACK PEPPER	

1 Preheat oven to 400°F. Heat large saucepot of water to boiling on high.

2 Finely chop one-third of parsley. Rub chopped parsley and rosemary all over tenderloin and let stand while oven heats.

3 Fill large bowl with ice and water. Add carrots to boiling water. Cook 5 minutes. With tongs, transfer to ice water. When cool, remove with tongs to cutting board. Add asparagus to boiling water. Cook 3 minutes or until bright green and tender-crisp. Transfer to ice water. When cool, drain well.

4 Sprinkle ⅛ teaspoon each salt and pepper all over pork. In ovenproof 12-inch skillet, heat 1 teaspoon oil on medium-high heat. Add pork; cook 6 to 8 minutes or until evenly browned, turning. Transfer to oven. Roast 8 to 10 minutes or until instant-read thermometer inserted in thickest part of pork registers 145°F; let rest 5 minutes.

5 While pork cooks, cut carrots into 2-inch-long matchsticks. Cut asparagus into 2-inch-long pieces. In large bowl, toss carrots, asparagus, radishes, green onion, baby greens, and remaining parsley with remaining ⅛ teaspoon each salt and pepper as well as remaining 1 tablespoon oil. Add balsamic vinegar; toss to combine. Divide salad among serving plates. Slice pork; arrange on top of salads.

EACH SERVING: ABOUT 235 CALORIES | 26G PROTEIN | 14G CARBOHYDRATE | 8G TOTAL FAT (2G SATURATED) | 5G FIBER | 62MG CHOLESTEROL | 255MG SODIUM ☺ ♥

PORK CHOPS WITH PEPPERS AND ONION

Boneless chops are smothered in green onions and red peppers for this fast and easy skillet dinner. Add a side of steamed spinach or zucchini, if you like.

ACTIVE TIME: 10 MINUTES · **TOTAL TIME:** 30 MINUTES

MAKES: 4 MAIN-DISH SERVINGS

---

4 BONELESS PORK LOIN CHOPS, ½ INCH THICK (4 OUNCES EACH), TRIMMED

½ TEASPOON SALT

¼ TEASPOON GROUND BLACK PEPPER

2 TEASPOONS OLIVE OIL

1 BUNCH GREEN ONIONS, GREEN TOPS CUT DIAGONALLY INTO 3-INCH PIECES, WHITE BOTTOMS THINLY SLICED CROSSWISE

2 RED PEPPERS, CUT INTO 1½-INCH PIECES

1 GARLIC CLOVE, CRUSHED WITH GARLIC PRESS

⅛ TEASPOON CRUSHED RED PEPPER

½ CUP CHICKEN BROTH

1 Heat nonstick 12-inch skillet over medium heat until hot but not smoking. Add pork chops to skillet and sprinkle with salt and pepper. Cook until lightly browned outside and still slightly pink inside, about 8 minutes, turning over once; reduce heat to medium if chops are browning too quickly. (Instant-read thermometer inserted horizontally into center of chops should register 145°F.) Transfer chops to plate; keep warm.

2 To same skillet over medium heat, add oil and green-onion tops; cook 4 minutes. With slotted spoon, transfer green-onion tops to small bowl. In same skillet, cook red peppers and green-onion bottoms, stirring occasionally, 8 to 10 minutes. Add garlic and crushed red pepper, and cook, stirring, 1 minute. Stir in broth and half of green-onion tops; heat through. Spoon pepper mixture onto platter; arrange pork and remaining green-onion tops on peppers.

EACH SERVING: ABOUT 210 CALORIES | 26G PROTEIN | 7G CARBOHYDRATE | 8G TOTAL FAT (2G SATURATED) | 2G FIBER | 71MG CHOLESTEROL | 495MG SODIUM 💚 😊

PORK CHOPS WITH TOMATO AND ARUGULA SALAD

Prepare this delicious pork chop dinner, complete with salad, in just fifteen minutes!

ACTIVE TIME: 10 MINUTES · **TOTAL TIME:** 15 MINUTES

MAKES: 4 MAIN-DISH SERVINGS

⅓ CUP PLAIN DRIED BREAD CRUMBS

¼ CUP GRATED ROMANO CHEESE

1 TEASPOON SALT

1 LARGE EGG

4 BONELESS PORK LOIN CHOPS, ½-INCH THICK (4 OUNCES EACH)

2 TABLESPOONS OLIVE OIL

1 TABLESPOON FRESH LEMON JUICE

1 BAG (4 TO 5 OUNCES) BABY ARUGULA

½ SMALL RED ONION, THINLY SLICED

1 LARGE RIPE TOMATO (12 OUNCES), COARSELY CHOPPED

1 On waxed paper, combine bread crumbs, Romano, and ½ teaspoon salt. In pie plate, with fork, beat egg. Dip chops, one at a time, in egg, then in bread-crumb mixture to coat. Repeat with remaining chops.

2 In nonstick 12-inch skillet, heat 1 tablespoon oil over medium heat. Add chops and cook until lightly browned outside and still slightly pink inside, 6 to 8 minutes, turning over once. (Instant-read thermometer inserted horizontally into center of chops should register 145°F.)

3 Meanwhile, in medium bowl, combine lemon juice and remaining 1 tablespoon oil and ½ teaspoon salt. Add arugula, onion, and tomato to bowl and toss to coat with dressing.

4 Transfer chops to dinner plates; top with salad.

EACH SERVING: ABOUT 370 CALORIES | 31G PROTEIN | 14G CARBOHYDRATE | 22G TOTAL FAT (6G SATURATED) | 2G FIBER | 128MG CHOLESTEROL | 800MG SODIUM ◔ ☺

CUBAN MOJO PORK CHOPS

Mojo (pronounced MO-ho) comes from the Spanish verb mojar, "to wet." This seasoning mix is an integral component of Latin cuisine, traditionally made with citrus juice, garlic, salt, and lard. Updated versions using spices, chiles, and other fruit make it extremely versatile. Serve with a salad of Boston lettuce, avocado (one serves four), and chopped red onion tossed with lime juice and olive oil.

ACTIVE TIME: 15 MINUTES · **TOTAL TIME:** 30 MINUTES PLUS MARINATING

MAKES: 4 MAIN-DISH SERVINGS

2	NAVEL ORANGES	4	GARLIC CLOVES
¼	CUP CHOPPED ONION	2	TABLESPOONS FRESH LIME JUICE
¼	CUP RED WINE VINEGAR	¼	TEASPOON SALT
1	CHIPOTLE CHILE IN ADOBO PLUS 1 TABLESPOON ADOBO (SEE TIP, PAGE 60)	4	PORK LOIN CHOPS, ¾ INCH THICK (8 OUNCES EACH), TRIMMED

1 From oranges, grate ½ teaspoon peel and squeeze ½ cup juice.

2 In blender or food processor with knife blade attached, pulse orange peel, onion, vinegar, chipotle chile, adobo, and garlic until pureed.

3 Pour marinade into large resealable plastic bag; stir in orange and lime juices and salt. Add pork chops to marinade, turning to coat. Seal bag, pressing out excess air. Place bag on plate; let stand 15 minutes at room temperature or 1 hour in the refrigerator, turning over several times.

4 Prepare outdoor grill for direct grilling over medium heat.

5 Remove chops from bag; pour marinade into 1-quart saucepan and reserve. Place chops on hot grill rack. Cover and grill chops until lightly browned outside and still slightly pink inside, 6 to 8 minutes per side. (Instant-read thermometer inserted horizontally into center of chops should register 145°F.)

6 Meanwhile, heat reserved marinade to boiling over high heat; boil 2 minutes. Serve pork chops drizzled with cooked marinade.

EACH SERVING: ABOUT 395 CALORIES | 42G PROTEIN | 10G CARBOHYDRATE | 19G TOTAL FAT (7G SATURATED) | 1G FIBER | 116MG CHOLESTEROL | 410MG SODIUM

MIDDLE EASTERN LAMB STEAKS

Aromatic spices—thyme, coriander, cumin, and allspice—in a quick tomato relish add zip to pan-seared lamb steaks. See "Meze in Minutes," opposite, for easy low-carb add-ons to round out the meal.

ACTIVE TIME: 15 MINUTES · **TOTAL TIME:** 35 MINUTES

MAKES: 4 MAIN-DISH SERVINGS

1	TEASPOON DRIED THYME	1	RED ONION, CHOPPED
1	TEASPOON GROUND CORIANDER	¼	CUP DRIED CURRANTS
1	TEASPOON GROUND CUMIN	1	TABLESPOON PINE NUTS (PIGNOLI; OPTIONAL)
½	TEASPOON GROUND ALLSPICE		
½	TEASPOON SALT	2	TABLESPOONS CHOPPED FRESH PARSLEY LEAVES
¼	TEASPOON GROUND BLACK PEPPER		
1	CAN (28 OUNCES) WHOLE TOMATOES	2	CENTER-CUT LAMB LEG STEAKS, ¾ INCH THICK (8 OUNCES EACH), TRIMMED
1	TEASPOON VEGETABLE OIL		

1 In small bowl, stir together thyme, coriander, cumin, allspice, salt, and pepper. Drain tomatoes, reserving ½ cup juice; chop tomatoes.

2 In nonstick 12-inch skillet, heat oil over medium heat until hot. Add onion and 2 teaspoons thyme mixture. Cook, stirring occasionally, until onion is slightly softened, 5 minutes. Add chopped tomatoes, reserved juice, and currants. Cook, stirring occasionally, until slightly thickened, 6 minutes. Transfer tomato mixture to bowl; stir in pine nuts, if using, and 1 tablespoon chopped parsley.

3 Coat lamb steaks with remaining thyme mixture. In same skillet, cook lamb over medium heat 4 to 5 minutes per side for medium-rare or to desired doneness. (Instant-read thermometer inserted horizontally into center of steaks should register 145°F.) Cut each steak in half.

4 To serve, spoon tomato relish into deep platter; top with lamb and sprinkle with remaining 1 tablespoon parsley.

EACH SERVING: ABOUT 255 CALORIES | 26G PROTEIN | 17G CARBOHYDRATE | 9G TOTAL FAT (3G SATURATED) | 3G FIBER | 78MG CHOLESTEROL | 555MG SODIUM ☺

MEZE IN MINUTES

A tradition in the Middle East, Greece, and Turkey, meze are little savory dishes to be nibbled before a meal with drinks. Choose from the following low-carb options paired with sliced cucumbers, radishes, or ripe tomato wedges, if you like.

• Olives tossed with chopped fresh oregano, garlic, and lemon zest. Choose green olives, which contain just 1 gram carbs per ½ cup (compared to 4½ grams for black olives).

• Prepared hummus drizzled with olive oil and sprinkled with cayenne (ground red) pepper (4 grams carbs per 2 tablespoons).

• Prepared babaganoush or seasoned roasted eggplant dip (3 grams carbs in a 1-ounce serving).

• Stuffed grape leaves, purchased from a Middle Eastern market or at the deli counter of your supermarket (2 grams carbs per piece).

• Wedge of feta cheese drizzled with olive oil and sprinkled with chopped fresh mint (1 gram carbs in a 1-ounce serving).

• Roasted red peppers, available jarred or see our recipe for homemade on page 91 (2 grams carbs in ¼ cup pepper strips).

MUSHROOM GLAZED PORK CHOPS WITH GREEN BEANS

Everyday easy, these golden-crusted chops are quick-seared on the stove, roasted in a roaring oven, and topped with a silky cognac-and-cream sauce. Pair them with our tarragon-scented Brown Butter Green Beans (recipe opposite), as shown in the photo on page 2.

ACTIVE TIME: 20 MINUTES · **TOTAL TIME:** 40 MINUTES
MAKES: 4 MAIN-DISH SERVINGS

10	OUNCES CREMINI MUSHROOMS, TRIMMED AND QUARTERED	4	BONELESS, CENTER-CUT PORK LOIN CHOPS (EACH 6 OUNCES, 1-INCH THICK)
8	OUNCES FRESH SHIITAKE MUSHROOMS, STEMS DISCARDED, CUT INTO 1-INCH PIECES IF LARGE	1	TABLESPOON VEGETABLE OIL
		1	MEDIUM ONION (6 TO 8 OUNCES), FINELY CHOPPED
2	GARLIC CLOVES, VERY THINLY SLICED	¼	CUP COGNAC
1	TABLESPOON PLUS 1 TEASPOON SHERRY VINEGAR	¼	CUP LIGHT CREAM
½	TEASPOON FRESHLY GROUND BLACK PEPPER	½	TEASPOON SALT
		2	FRESH SAGE LEAVES, THINLY SLICED

1 Arrange oven racks in upper and lower thirds of oven. Preheat to 450°F.

2 In 15½" by 10½" jelly-roll pan, spread mushrooms in even layer. Sprinkle garlic on top. Roast on upper rack 15 minutes or until mushrooms are tender, juices are released, and garlic is golden brown.

3 Meanwhile, in 9-inch pie plate or other shallow dish, mix sugar, 1 tablespoon vinegar, and ¼ teaspoon pepper. Add pork and turn to evenly coat. There should be no excess liquid remaining.

4 Heat ovenproof 12-inch skillet on medium-high heat. Add oil to pan and swirl to coat bottom evenly. When oil shimmers and is almost smoking, add pork. Cook 1 to 2 minutes or until browned, then turn pork over and cook 2 minutes longer. Transfer to lower oven rack.

5 Roast 7 to 10 minutes or until barely pink in center. (Instant-read thermometer inserted horizontally into chop should register 145°F.) Transfer to plate; let rest.

6 To same skillet, add onion. Cook on medium heat 5 minutes or until browned, stirring occasionally. Add cognac and remaining 1 teaspoon vinegar and cook 30 seconds. Add mushroom mixture with any juices and reduce heat to low.

7 While stirring, add cream in slow, steady stream. Stir in ½ teaspoon salt and remaining ¼ teaspoon pepper. When mixture bubbles, remove from heat.
8 Divide pork chops and their juices among serving plates. Spoon mushroom mixture over pork; garnish with sage.

EACH SERVING: ABOUT 430 CALORIES | 39G PROTEIN | 16G CARBOHYDRATE | 22G TOTAL FAT (7G SATURATED) | 2G FIBER | 127MG CHOLESTEROL | 400MG SODIUM ☺

BROWN BUTTER GREEN BEANS

Browned butter imparts a unique nutty flavor to the beans; don't be tempted to substitute margarine or oil for it. This vegetable side dish is the perfect mate for our Mushroom Glazed Pork Chops.

ACTIVE TIME: 15 MINUTES · **TOTAL TIME:** 40 MINUTES
MAKES: 4 SIDE-DISH SERVINGS

1⅛	TEASPOON SALT	1	TABLESPOON FRESH TARRAGON LEAVES
1	POUND GREEN BEANS, TRIMMED	½	TEASPOON FRESH LEMON JUICE
2	TABLESPOONS BUTTER (NO SUBSTITUTIONS)	¼	TEASPOON FRESHLY GROUND BLACK PEPPER

1 Heat large covered saucepot of *water* to boiling on high heat. Fill large bowl with ice and water.
2 Add 1 teaspoon salt, then green beans, to boiling water. Cook, uncovered, 5 to 7 minutes or until tender-crisp. Drain and immediately transfer to bowl of ice water. When cool, drain again. Roll between paper towels to dry. Beans can be refrigerated in an airtight container or resealable plastic bag up to 3 days.
3 If serving immediately, in same saucepot, melt butter on low heat. When butter is melted, raise heat to medium and cook 3 to 4 minutes or until golden brown and aromatic, stirring and scraping pot. Add beans and cook 2 minutes or until glazed and heated through, tossing.
4 Remove from heat; toss with tarragon, lemon juice, remaining ⅛ teaspoon salt, and pepper.

EACH SERVING: ABOUT 85 CALORIES | 2G PROTEIN | 7G CARBOHYDRATE | 6G TOTAL FAT (4G SATURATED) | 3G FIBER | 15MG CHOLESTEROL | 120MG SODIUM ☺ 🗓

KANSAS CITY RIBS

Baby back ribs with a gooey tomato-based sauce are a summertime tradition. Pair with a simple slaw of shredded cabbage tossed with mayonnaise and white vinegar as shown in photo. You can even enjoy a frosty 12-ounce beer: Try low-carb options like Busch Light or Anheuser-Busch Natural Light and the total carbs for the meal will come in under 25.

ACTIVE TIME: 15 MINUTES · **TOTAL TIME:** 1 HOUR 30 MINUTES
MAKES: 6 MAIN-DISH SERVINGS

BABY BACK RIBS

3   RACKS PORK BABY BACK RIBS (1 POUND EACH)
1   ONION, CUT INTO QUARTERS
1   NAVEL ORANGE, CUT INTO QUARTERS
1   TABLESPOON WHOLE BLACK PEPPERCORNS
1   TABLESPOON WHOLE CORIANDER SEEDS

BARBECUE SAUCE

3   TABLESPOONS BUTTER OR MARGARINE
1   ONION, CHOPPED
4   GARLIC CLOVES, FINELY CHOPPED
1   CAN (15 OUNCES) TOMATO SAUCE
¼   CUP CIDER VINEGAR
ZERO-CALORIE SWEETENER (¼ CUP EQUIVALENT)
1   TEASPOON SALT
¼   TEASPOON COARSELY GROUND BLACK PEPPER

1 Prepare baby back ribs: In 8-quart saucepot, place ribs, onion, orange, peppercorns, coriander, and enough *water* to cover; heat to boiling on high. Reduce heat to low; partially cover and cook 50 minutes to 1 hour or until ribs are fork-tender. Transfer ribs to platter. If not serving right away, cover and refrigerate until ready to serve.

2 Meanwhile, prepare barbecue sauce: In 2-quart saucepan, heat butter over medium until melted. Add onion and garlic and cook until softened, stirring occasionally, 8 minutes. Add tomato sauce, vinegar, sweetener, salt, and pepper; heat to boiling on high. Reduce heat to low; simmer until thickened, stirring occasionally, 20 to 30 minutes. Makes about 2⅔ cups.

3 Prepare outdoor grill for direct grilling over medium heat.

4 Place ribs on hot grill rack. Cover and grill ribs until browned, 8 to 10 minutes, turning once. Brush ribs with some sauce and grill 5 to 10 minutes longer, brushing with remaining sauce and turning frequently.

5 To serve, cut racks into single-rib pieces and arrange on platter.

EACH SERVING: ABOUT 340 CALORIES | 21G PROTEIN | 4G CARBOHYDRATE | 27G TOTAL FAT (11G SATURATED) | 2G FIBER | 94MG CHOLESTEROL | 943MG SODIUM

CHILE-RUBBED HAM STEAK WITH PEACH SALSA

It's a quick grill—a fully cooked ham steak is patted with paprika and smoky chiles before searing. Our soothing fruit salsa tames the spice. Pair with a simple arugula and shaved jicama salad dressed with olive oil and fresh lime juice.

ACTIVE TIME: 30 MINUTES · **TOTAL TIME:** 35 MINUTES
MAKES: 4 MAIN-DISH SERVINGS

PEACH SALSA

4   RIPE PEACHES (1¼ POUNDS), PITTED AND CUT INTO ¼-INCH CHUNKS

1   CUP LOOSELY PACKED FRESH CILANTRO LEAVES, CHOPPED

1   JALAPEÑO CHILE, SEEDED AND MINCED

2   TABLESPOONS NO-SUGAR-ADDED PEACH JAM

2   TABLESPOONS FRESH LIME JUICE

¼   TEASPOON SALT

CHILE-RUBBED HAM

1   TABLESPOON PAPRIKA

1   TABLESPOON OLIVE OIL

2   TEASPOONS MINCED CHIPOTLE CHILE IN ADOBO OR 2 TEASPOONS ADOBO SAUCE (SEE TIP, PAGE 60)

1   FULLY COOKED CENTER-CUT HAM STEAK, ½ INCH THICK (1¼ POUNDS)

1 Prepare outdoor grill for direct grilling over medium-high heat.

2 Prepare peach salsa: In medium bowl, toss peaches, cilantro, jalapeño, jam, lime juice, and salt. Cover and refrigerate salsa up to 1 day if not serving right away. Makes about 4 cups.

3 Prepare chile-rubbed ham: In cup, mix paprika, oil, and chipotle chile. Spread mixture on both sides of ham.

4 Place ham on hot grill rack; grill, turning ham once, until lightly browned and heated through, 4 to 6 minutes. Serve ham with salsa.

EACH SERVING HAM WITH ½ CUP SALSA: ABOUT 220 CALORIES | 24G PROTEIN | 18G CARBOHYDRATE | 8G TOTAL FAT (2G SATURATED) | 72MG CHOLESTEROL | 1,900MG SODIUM ☺

APRICOT-MUSTARD GLAZED HAM

This glistening ham is a simple but worthy centerpiece for entertaining. Brussels sprouts roasted with olive oil, chopped walnuts, and fresh sage would make for a satisfying side—½ cup sprouts plus 1 tablespoon walnuts adds just 6 grams of carbs to the meal.

ACTIVE TIME: 15 MINUTES · **TOTAL TIME:** 1 HOUR 45 MINUTES PLUS STANDING

MAKES: 10 MAIN-DISH SERVINGS

1   FULLY COOKED SMOKED BONE-IN SHANK-HALF HAM (7 POUNDS)

⅓   CUP NO-SUGAR-ADDED APRICOT PRESERVES

1   TABLESPOON DIJON MUSTARD

1   Preheat oven to 325°F. If necessary, with sharp knife, remove skin and trim fat from ham, leaving about ¼-inch-thick layer of fat. Place ham in medium roasting pan (14" by 10"). Bake ham 1 hour.

2   In small bowl, stir apricot preserves and mustard until blended.

3   Remove ham from oven; brush with glaze. Return to oven and bake 25 to 30 minutes longer, until instant-read thermometer inserted into thickest part of ham, without touching bone, registers 140°F.

4   Transfer ham to warm platter and let stand 15 minutes to set juices for easier slicing. (Internal temperature of ham will rise 5°F to 10°F upon standing.)

EACH SERVING: ABOUT 235 CALORIES | 31G PROTEIN | 5G CARBOHYDRATE | 8G TOTAL FAT (3G SATURATED) | 0G FIBER | 71MG CHOLESTEROL | 1,750MG SODIUM ☺

CHINESE RED-COOKED PORK SHOULDER

Pork cooked in a slow cooker becomes so tender it almost melts in your mouth. This fragrant, Asian-style stew is simmered for hours in a combination of soy sauce, dry sherry, fresh ginger, and orange peel. Baby carrots and broccoli florets make it a complete one-pot meal.

ACTIVE TIME: 35 MINUTES · **SLOW-COOK TIME:** 8 HOURS 10 MINUTES ON LOW
MAKES: 10 MAIN-DISH SERVINGS

¼ CUP DRY SHERRY

¼ CUP RICE VINEGAR

5 TABLESPOONS REDUCED-SODIUM SOY SAUCE

1 ONION, CHOPPED

1 (2-INCH) PIECE FRESH GINGER, PEELED AND THINLY SLICED INTO ROUNDS

2 GARLIC CLOVES, CRUSHED WITH GARLIC PRESS

2 STRIPS (3" BY ¾" EACH) FRESH ORANGE PEEL

1 CINNAMON STICK (3 INCHES)

1 WHOLE STAR ANISE

1 BAG (1 POUND) PEELED BABY CARROTS

4 POUNDS WELL-TRIMMED BONELESS PORK SHOULDER, CUT INTO 1½-INCH CHUNKS (SEE TIP)

2 PACKAGES (10 OUNCES EACH) FROZEN BROCCOLI FLORETS, THAWED

1 In 6- to 6½-quart slow-cooker bowl, combine sherry, rice vinegar, and ¼ cup soy sauce. Stir in onion, ginger, garlic, orange peel, cinnamon, star anise, and carrots. Top with pork; do not stir. Cover slow cooker with lid and cook as manufacturer directs on Low 8 hours.

2 When pork has cooked 8 hours, open lid and stir in thawed broccoli. Cover and continue to cook until broccoli is heated through, about 10 minutes.

3 Discard cinnamon stick and star anise. Skim and discard fat from cooking liquid. Stir in remaining 1 tablespoon soy sauce.

TIP You want 4 pounds of solid meat. If the pork is not well trimmed when you buy it, purchase 4½ or 5 pounds so you'll have enough meat after you cut away the excess fat and skin.

EACH SERVING: ABOUT 320 CALORIES | 38G PROTEIN | 12G CARBOHYDRATE | 13G TOTAL FAT (4G SATURATED) | 2G FIBER | 121MG CHOLESTEROL | 645MG SODIUM 🙂 🍲 🍱

PORK AND POSOLE STEW

This is the Southwestern version of a traditional Mexican pork-and-hominy stew that's often served as a festive meal over the holidays. A staple of the Southwest's Pueblo Indians, posole—or hominy—is made with white or yellow corn kernels treated with slaked lime or lye until the kernels double in size. They're then degermed, hulled, washed, and dried. Our recipe uses convenient ready-to-eat canned hominy.

ACTIVE TIME: 45 MINUTES · **TOTAL TIME:** 2 HOURS 30 MINUTES

MAKES: 10 CUPS OR 10 MAIN-DISH SERVINGS

---

1 TABLESPOON OLIVE OIL

3 POUNDS BONELESS PORK SHOULDER BLADE ROAST (FRESH PORK BUTT), TRIMMED AND CUT INTO 2-INCH CHUNKS

1 LARGE ROASTED RED PEPPER (SEE BOX), OR 3½ OUNCES PREPARED ROASTED RED PEPPERS, DRAINED

¼ TEASPOON CAYENNE (GROUND RED) PEPPER

2 LARGE ONIONS (12 OUNCES EACH), CHOPPED

4 GARLIC CLOVES, CRUSHED WITH GARLIC PRESS

2 JALAPEÑO CHILES, SEEDED AND MINCED

1 CAN (14½ OUNCES) WHOLE TOMATOES

1½ TEASPOONS SALT

1 TEASPOON DRIED OREGANO

¼ TEASPOON COARSELY GROUND BLACK PEPPER

1 CUP WATER

1 CAN (29 OUNCES) HOMINY, RINSED AND DRAINED

SLICED RADISHES, CILANTRO LEAVES, AND DICED AVOCADO FOR GARNISH

---

1 In nonstick 5- or 6-quart saucepot or Dutch oven, heat 1 teaspoon oil on medium heat until very hot. Add one-third of pork; cook until browned on all sides, about 8 minutes, stirring often. With slotted spoon, transfer pork to bowl as it is browned. Repeat twice more with remaining pork, using 1 teaspoon oil per batch; set aside.

2 Meanwhile, place roasted red pepper in blender along with cayenne; blend until pureed.

3 To same saucepot, add onions, garlic, and jalapeños; cook until vegetables are tender, stirring occasionally, about 10 minutes.

4 Return pork to saucepot. Add tomatoes with their juice, salt, oregano, black pepper, pureed red-pepper mixture, and water; heat to boiling on medium-high heat, breaking up tomatoes with side of spoon. Reduce heat to low; cover and simmer until meat is fork-tender and cooked through, stirring occasionally, about 1 hour 30 minutes.

ROASTED RED PEPPERS

You can purchase these readymade, but it's easy enough to roast them yourself. If you're not using them right away, refrigerate in an airtight container up to 3 days or freeze up to 3 months.

Step 1: Preheat broiler and line broiling pan with foil. Cut each pepper lengthwise in half; remove and discard stems and seeds. Arrange peppers, cut side down, in prepared broiling pan. Place pan in broiler, 5 to 6 inches from heat source. Broil, without turning, until skin is charred and blistered, 8 to 10 minutes.

Step 2: Wrap peppers in foil and allow to steam at room temperature 15 minutes or until cool enough to handle.

Step 3: Remove peppers from foil. Peel skin and discard. Slice or chop as recipe directs.

5 Stir in hominy; cover and cook until heated through, about 15 minutes longer. Garnish each serving with radishes, cilantro, and avocado.

EACH SERVING: ABOUT 255 CALORIES | 24G PROTEIN | 14G CARBOHYDRATE | 11G TOTAL FAT (3G SATURATED) | 3G FIBER | 77MG CHOLESTEROL | 620MG SODIUM ☺ ▭

SPICE-BRINED PORK LOIN

Brining pork in a blend of kosher salt, sugar, and spices infuses it with flavor and keeps it tender and juicy. Allow the pork to soak in the brine for 18 to 24 hours before roasting. Serve with a side of sautéed garlicky greens or broccoli.

ACTIVE TIME: 20 MINUTES · **TOTAL TIME:** 1 HOUR 20 MINUTES PLUS BRINING AND STANDING · **MAKES:** 12 MAIN-DISH SERVINGS

2 CUPS COLD WATER

¼ CUP KOSHER SALT

2 TABLESPOONS CORIANDER SEEDS

2 TABLESPOONS CRACKED BLACK PEPPER

2 TABLESPOONS FENNEL SEEDS

2 TABLESPOONS CUMIN SEEDS

PEEL FROM 1 NAVEL ORANGE, WHITE PITH REMOVED

3 CUPS ICE

1 BONELESS PORK LOIN ROAST (3 POUNDS), TRIMMED

4 GARLIC CLOVES, CRUSHED WITH SIDE OF CHEF'S KNIFE

1 In 2-quart saucepan, heat 1 cup water, salt, coriander, pepper, fennel, cumin, and orange peel to boiling over high heat. Reduce heat to low; simmer 2 minutes. Remove saucepan from heat; stir in ice until almost melted. Stir in remaining 1 cup water.

2 Place pork with garlic in large resealable plastic bag and brine. Seal bag, pressing out excess air. Place bag in bowl or small roasting pan and refrigerate 18 to 24 hours.

3 Preheat oven to 400°F. Remove pork from bag; discard brine (it's okay if some spices stick to pork). Place pork on rack in medium roasting pan (14" by 10"). Roast until thermometer inserted into thickest part of meat reaches 145°F, 1 hour to 1 hour 15 minutes (temperature will rise 5°F to 10°F upon standing). Transfer pork to cutting board and let stand 10 minutes to set juices for easier slicing.

EACH SERVING: ABOUT 175 CALORIES | 24G PROTEIN | 1G CARBOHYDRATE | 8G TOTAL FAT (3G SATURATED) | 0G FIBER | 67MG CHOLESTEROL | 445MG SODIUM ☺ ♥

SOPRESSATA AND ROMA BEAN SALAD WITH PECORINO

This antipasto-style salad is hearty enough to make a meal. Look for Roma beans, a flat Italian snap bean, in the farmer's market or speciality Italian grocers during the summer months. If not available, green beans make a tasty swap.

ACTIVE TIME: 10 MINUTES · **TOTAL TIME:** 20 MINUTES
MAKES: 4 MAIN-DISH SERVINGS

1¼ POUNDS ROMA (BROAD) BREANS, TRIMMED

1 LEMON

2 TABLESPOONS EXTRA-VIRGIN OLIVE OIL

¼ TEASPOON SALT

⅛ TEASPOON COARSELY GROUND BLACK PEPPER

4 OUNCES THINLY SLICED SOPRESSATA OR GENOA SALAMI, CUT INTO ½-INCH-WIDE STRIPS

2 BUNCHES ARUGULA (4 OUNCES EACH), TOUGH STEMS DISCARDED

1 SMALL WEDGE PECORINO-ROMANO CHEESE (2 OUNCES)

1 If Roma beans are very long, cut crosswise, on a diagononal, into 2½-inch pieces. In 12-inch skillet, heat 1 inch *water* to boiling over high. Add beans; heat to boiling. Reduce heat to low; simmer until beans are tender-crisp, 6 to 8 minutes. Drain beans. Rinse with cold running water to stop cooking; drain again.

2 Meanwhile, from lemon, grate ½ teaspoon peel and squeeze 2 table-spoons juice. In large bowl, with wire whisk, mix lemon peel and juice with oil, salt, and pepper.

3 Add beans, sopressata, and arugula to dressing in bowl; toss to coat.

4 To serve, spoon salad onto platter. With vegetable peeler, shave thin strips from wedge of Pecorino to top salad.

EACH SERVING: ABOUT 280 CLAORIES | 14G PROTEIN | 14G CARBOHYDRATE | 21G TOTAL FAT (7G SATURATED) | 5G FIBER | 41MG CHOLESTEROL | 845MG SODIUM ◐ ☺

BUTTERFLIED LAMB WITH MOROCCAN FLAVORS

This grilled leg of lamb features fabulous exotic flavor and requires very little work. Serve a simple tabbouleh featuring ½ cup cooked couscous tossed with ½ cup chopped ripe tomato, 1 cup chopped fresh parsley, olive oil, and lemon juice. Total carbs for the meal comes in at 25 grams.

ACTIVE TIME: 15 MINUTES · **TOTAL TIME:** 30 MINUTES PLUS MARINATING

MAKES: 12 MAIN-DISH SERVINGS

⅓ CUP LOOSELY PACKED FRESH CILANTRO LEAVES, CHOPPED

¼ CUP OLIVE OIL

2 TABLESPOONS DRIED MINT

2 TEASPOONS GROUND CORIANDER

1 TEASPOON GROUND GINGER

1 TEASPOON SALT

½ TEASPOON COARSELY GROUND BLACK PEPPER

½ TEASPOON CHILI POWDER

3½ POUNDS BUTTERFLIED BONELESS LAMB LEG, TRIMMED (SEE TIP)

1 In small bowl, stir together cilantro, oil, mint, coriander, ginger, salt, pepper, and chili powder.

2 Place lamb in 13" by 9" baking dish. Rub with cilantro mixture to coat completely. Cover and refrigerate at least 1 hour or up to 4 hours.

3 Prepare outdoor grill for direct grilling over medium-low heat.

4 Place lamb on hot grill rack. Cover and grill lamb 15 to 25 minutes for medium-rare or to desired doneness, turning lamb over occasionally. (Instant-read thermometer should register 145°F.) Thickness of butterflied lamb will vary throughout; cut off sections as meat is cooked through and transfer to cutting board.

5 Let lamb stand 10 minutes to allow juices to set for easier slicing. Thinly slice lamb to serve.

TIP You can ask your butcher to debone a 4½-pound half lamb leg shank and slit the meat lengthwise so that it opens like a thick steak.

EACH SERVING: ABOUT 225 CALORIES | 28G PROTEIN | 1G CARBOHYDRATE | 12G TOTAL FAT (3G SATURATED) | 0G FIBER | 88MG CHOLESTEROL | 270MG SODIUM ☺ ♥

SPICY GARLIC LAMB WITH CUCUMBER RAITA

Leg of lamb is divine cooked on the grill. Cucumbers in a minted yogurt dressing balance the spicy meat. Serve with a mix of grilled eggplant, red peppers, and yellow squash to add great flavor and color to your plate.

ACTIVE TIME: 30 MINUTES · **TOTAL TIME:** 45 MINUTES PLUS CHILLING AND STANDING
MAKES: 8 MAIN-DISH SERVINGS

CUCUMBER RAITA

1½ POUNDS KIRBY CUCUMBERS

1   TEASPOON SALT

2   CUPS PLAIN LOW-FAT YOGURT

½   CUP LOOSELY PACKED FRESH MINT LEAVES, CHOPPED

SPICED LAMB

1   TABLESPOON FENNEL SEEDS

1   TABLESPOON MUSTARD SEEDS

1   TABLESPOON CUMIN SEEDS

2   TEASPOONS SALT

1   TEASPOON WHOLE BLACK PEPPERCORNS

1   TEASPOON DRIED THYME LEAVES

3   WHOLE CLOVES

3   GARLIC CLOVES, CRUSHED WITH GARLIC PRESS

2   TABLESPOONS FRESH LEMON JUICE

3½ POUNDS BUTTERFLIED BONELESS LAMB LEG, TRIMMED (SEE TIP, PAGE 95)

1 Prepare cucumber raita: With vegetable peeler, remove several strips of peel from each cucumber. Cut each cucumber lengthwise in half; scoop out seeds. Cut each half lengthwise in half, then crosswise into ½-inch-thick pieces. In medium bowl, toss cucumbers with ¼ teaspoon salt; let stand 10 minutes. With hand, press cucumbers to remove as much liquid as possible; drain. Stir in yogurt, mint, and remaining ¾ teaspoon salt. Cover and refrigerate until ready to serve or up to 6 hours. Makes about 4 cups.

2 Prepare outdoor grill for direct grilling over medium-low heat.

3 Prepare spiced lamb: In spice grinder or coffee grinder, blend fennel, mustard, cumin, salt, peppercorns, thyme, and cloves until finely ground. In small bowl, mix garlic and lemon juice with ground spices until blended. Rub spice mixture over both sides of lamb.

4 Place lamb on hot grill rack. Cover and grill 15 to 25 minutes for medium-rare or to desired doneness, turning lamb over once. (Instant-read thermometer should register 145°F.) Thickness of butterflied lamb will vary throughout; cut off sections as meat is cooked and place on cutting board. Let lamb stand 10 minutes to set juices for easier slicing. Thinly slice lamb and arrange on platter. Serve with cucumber raita.

EACH SERVING LAMB WITH ½ CUP RAITA: ABOUT 335 CALORIES | 43G PROTEIN | 12G CARBOHYDRATE | 13G TOTAL FAT (4G SATURATED) | 3G FIBER | 125MG CHOLESTEROL | 935MG SODIUM ☺

SEAFOOD

Seafood is a rich source of protein and low in fat, making it an ideal candidate for low-carb meals. Fresh herbs, zippy marinades, and salad greens dress up dishes like Ginger-Shallot Cod on Watercress. Recipes for cold-water fish like Salmon with Tomato-Olive Relish deliver tons of flavor plus essential fatty acids. Start serving seafood at least one night a week!

KEY TO ICONS

◔ 30 minutes or less   ☺ Low calorie   ♥ Heart healthy   🍲 Make ahead   🍲 Slow cooker

Shrimp and Tomato Summer Salad (page 120)

FISHERMAN'S STEW

Fennel and tomato accent the seafood trio of cod, shrimp, and mussels in this satisfying meal. Double this one when company's coming—just make sure to use a large Dutch oven instead of a skillet.

ACTIVE TIME: 30 MINUTES · **TOTAL TIME:** 55 MINUTES
MAKES: 4 MAIN-DISH SERVINGS

2 TEASPOONS OLIVE OIL	½ CUP DRY WHITE WINE
1 ONION, CHOPPED	1 CAN (14½ OUNCES) DICED TOMATOES
1 POUND FENNEL BULB, TRIMMED, CORED, AND THINLY SLICED	1 POUND COD FILLETS, CUT INTO 1¼-INCH PIECES
½ TEASPOON SALT	1 POUND MUSSELS, SCRUBBED AND DEBEARDED
⅛ TEASPOON COARSELY GROUND BLACK PEPPER	8 OUNCES LARGE SHRIMP, SHELLED AND DEVEINED (SEE BOX, PAGE 120), TAIL LEFT ON, IF YOU LIKE
1 LARGE LEMON	
2 GARLIC CLOVES, CRUSHED WITH GARLIC PRESS	½ CUP LOOSELY PACKED FRESH PARSLEY LEAVES, CHOPPED, FOR GARNISH
1 BOTTLE (8 OUNCES) CLAM JUICE	

1 In deep nonstick 12-inch skillet, heat oil over medium heat until hot. Add onion, fennel, salt, and pepper; cook, covered, 10 minutes, stirring occasionally, until vegetables are tender and golden.

2 Meanwhile, from lemon, with vegetable peeler, remove 3 strips peel (3" by ¾" each).

3 Add garlic to skillet and cook 30 seconds. Add clam juice, wine, and lemon peel; heat to boiling. Boil 1 minute. Reduce heat to medium-low and simmer, stirring occasionally, 5 minutes.

4 Stir in tomatoes with their juice; heat to boiling over medium-high heat. Add cod, mussels, and shrimp; heat to boiling. Reduce heat to medium-low and simmer, covered, until fish and shrimp turn opaque throughout and mussel shells open, 6 to 7 minutes.

5 Discard lemon peel and any mussels that have not opened. Sprinkle with chopped parsley just before serving.

EACH SERVING: ABOUT 265 CALORIES | 34G PROTEIN | 17G CARBOHYDRATE | 6G TOTAL FAT (1G SATURATED) | 4G FIBER | 111MG CHOLESTEROL | 1,145MG SODIUM ☺ 🍲

COD WITH BACON AND CABBAGE

Cabbage is cooked with bacon and seasonings, then topped with cod in this easy four-ingredient dinner. You can substitute other firm white fish fillets such as orange roughy, pollock, or halibut for the cod.

ACTIVE TIME: 15 MINUTES · **TOTAL TIME:** 40 MINUTES
MAKES: 4 MAIN-DISH SERVINGS

2   SLICES BACON, CHOPPED

1   SMALL SAVOY CABBAGE (2 POUNDS), THINLY SLICED (12 CUPS)

⅛   TEASPOON DRIED THYME

½   TEASPOON SALT

¼   TEASPOON COARSELY GROUND BLACK PEPPER

2   TABLESPOONS WATER

4   COD FILLETS, ¾ INCH THICK EACH (6 OUNCES EACH)

1 In nonstick 12-inch skillet, cook bacon over medium heat until browned, about 5 minutes, stirring frequently. With slotted spoon, transfer bacon to paper towels to drain. Discard all but 2 teaspoons bacon fat from skillet.

2 To same skillet, add cabbage, thyme, ¼ teaspoon salt, ⅛ teaspoon pepper, and water. Cook over medium-high heat 5 to 8 minutes or until cabbage is wilted, stirring frequently. Stir in bacon.

3 Top cabbage mixture with cod fillets. Sprinkle cod with remaining ¼ teaspoon salt and ⅛ teaspoon pepper. Cover skillet and cook over medium heat 10 to 12 minutes or until cod is opaque throughout. (Instant-read thermometer inserted horizontally into center of cod should register 145°F.)

EACH SERVING: ABOUT 235 CALORIES | 36G PROTEIN | 13G CARBOHYDRATE | 5G TOTAL FAT (2G SATURATED) | 7G FIBER | 78MG CHOLESTEROL | 490MG SODIUM ☺

STEAMED SAVORY HALIBUT

Mild and meaty, halibut gets instant oomph from slow steaming with cayenne—and a garden-ripe garnish of briny green olives, corn, and tomatoes. Chives and mint add a final flurry of color.

ACTIVE TIME: 20 MINUTES · **TOTAL TIME:** 30 MINUTES

MAKES: 4 MAIN-DISH SERVINGS

4	SKINLESS HALIBUT OR COD FILLETS (6 OUNCES EACH)	2	TABLESPOONS EXTRA-VIRGIN OLIVE OIL
1	PINCH CAYENNE (GROUND RED) PEPPER	1	SMALL SHALLOT, FINELY CHOPPED
½	TEASPOON SALT	1½	CUPS FRESH CORN KERNELS
1	POUND PLUM TOMATOES, CHOPPED	2	TABLESPOONS SNIPPED FRESH CHIVES, PLUS ADDITIONAL FOR GARNISH
½	CUP PITTED GREEN OLIVES, THINLY SLICED (SEE TIP)	1	TABLESPOON FINELY CHOPPED FRESH MINT LEAVES, PLUS ADDITIONAL FOR GARNISH
1	TABLESPOON CHAMPAGNE VINEGAR		
1	TABLESPOON FRESH LEMON JUICE		

1 Fill 5-quart saucepot with 1 inch water. Fit a steamer insert or basket into saucepot. (Water should not touch bottom of steamer.) Cover and heat to boiling, then reduce heat to low to maintain very gentle simmer.

2 Sprinkle fish with cayenne and ¼ teaspoon salt to season both sides. Place fish in single layer in steamer. Cover and steam 20 minutes or until opaque throughout.

3 Meanwhile, in large bowl, combine tomatoes, olives, vinegar, lemon juice, 1 tablespoon oil, and remaining ¼ teaspoon salt. Set aside.

4 In 12-inch skillet, heat remaining 1 tablespoon oil on medium-high heat. Add shallot and cook 1 minute or until browned, stirring. Add corn and cook 2 to 3 minutes or until browned, stirring occasionally. Transfer to bowl with tomato mixture. Add chives and mint and stir until well mixed.

5 Divide tomato mixture among serving plates. Remove steamer from saucepot. Carefully remove fish from steamer and place on top of tomato mixture on each plate. Garnish with chives and mint; serve immediately.

TIP For this recipe, we prefer the assertiveness of briny green olives (not ripe green olives) found at your supermarket's deli bar.

EACH SERVING: ABOUT 360 CALORIES | 42G PROTEIN | 17G CARBOHYDRATE | 14G TOTAL FAT (2G SATURATED) | 3G FIBER | 68MG CHOLESTEROL | 640MG SODIUM 🙂 ☺

THAI SNAPPER IN FOIL PACKETS

Tender fillets seasoned with lime and ginger are cooked in a foil packet for ease. This helps to seal in the juices, too. Pair with ½ cup steamed edamame beans.

ACTIVE TIME: 20 MINUTES · **TOTAL TIME:** 30 MINUTES
MAKES: 4 MAIN-DISH SERVINGS

---

3 TABLESPOONS FRESH LIME JUICE
1 TABLESPOON SUGAR-FREE ASIAN FISH SAUCE (SEE TIP, PAGE 21)
1 TABLESPOON OLIVE OIL
1 TEASPOON GRATED, PEELED FRESH GINGER
½ TEASPOON MINCED GARLIC
4 RED SNAPPER FILLETS (6 OUNCES EACH)
1 LARGE CARROT, PEELED AND CUT INTO 2¼-INCH-LONG MATCHSTICK-THIN STRIPS
1 GREEN ONION, THINLY SLICED
¼ CUP PACKED FRESH CILANTRO LEAVES

1 Prepare outdoor grill for direct grilling over medium heat.
2 In small bowl, mix lime juice, fish sauce, olive oil, ginger, and garlic.
3 From roll of foil, cut four 16" by 12" sheets. Fold each sheet crosswise in half and open up again.
4 Place 1 red snapper fillet, skin side down, on half of each piece of foil. Top with carrot strips, green onion slices, then cilantro leaves. Spoon lime-juice mixture over snapper and vegetables. Fold other half of foil over fish. Fold and crimp foil edges all around to create sealed packets.
5 Place packets on hot grill rack; grill 8 minutes, until fish flakes easily when tested with fork.
6 To serve, with kitchen shears, cut X in top of each packet so steam can escape, then transfer each fillet to plate.

EACH SERVING: ABOUT 220 CALORIES | 36G PROTEIN | 5G CARBOHYDRATE | 6G TOTAL FAT (1G SATURATED) | 1G FIBER | 62MG CHOLESTEROL | 445MG SODIUM

FLOUNDER PESTO ROLL-UPS

Fresh fish fillets are spread with store-bought pesto and baked with white wine and plum tomatoes for a simply satisfying meal. Roast broccoli florets tossed with pine nuts and grated Parmesan alongside the fish; a ½ cup serving with 1 tablespoon pine nuts adds just 7 grams of carbs to the meal.

ACTIVE TIME: 15 MINUTES · **TOTAL TIME:** 35 MINUTES

MAKES: 4 MAIN-DISH SERVINGS

4 FLOUNDER FILLETS (6 OUNCES EACH)	4 PLUM TOMATOES, CHOPPED
8 TEASPOONS PREPARED BASIL PESTO	¼ CUP LOOSELY PACKED FRESH PARSLEY LEAVES, CHOPPED, FOR GARNISH
¼ TEASPOON SALT	
¼ CUP DRY WHITE WINE	

1   Preheat oven to 400°F. Place fillets, skin sides down, on work surface. Spread 2 teaspoons pesto on each fillet; sprinkle with salt. Starting at narrow end of each fillet, roll up jelly-roll fashion. Place rolls, seam sides down, in 8-inch-square glass baking dish.

2   Pour wine over fillets and top with tomatoes. Cover dish and bake 20 minutes or until fish flakes easily when tested with fork. (Instant-read thermometer inserted horizontally into center of fillet should register 145°F.) Sprinkle with parsley to serve.

EACH SERVING: ABOUT 205 CALORIES | 31G PROTEIN | 5G CARBOHYDRATE | 6G TOTAL FAT (1G SATURATED) | 1G FIBER | 76MG CHOLESTEROL | 335MG SODIUM ☺ ♥

STEAMED SCROD FILLETS

These fresh fillets are steamed on a bed of bok choy and carrots with a drizzle of a ginger-soy mixture.

ACTIVE TIME: 15 MINUTES · **TOTAL TIME:** 25 MINUTES
MAKES: 4 MAIN-DISH SERVINGS

---

3   TABLESPOONS REDUCED-SODIUM SOY SAUCE

2   TABLESPOONS RICE VINEGAR

1   TABLESPOON FINELY CHOPPED, PEELED FRESH GINGER

1   GARLIC CLOVE, CRUSHED WITH GARLIC PRESS

1   POUND BOK CHOY, COARSELY CHOPPED

1¾ CUPS SHREDDED CARROTS

4   SCROD FILLETS (6 OUNCES EACH)

3   GREEN ONIONS, SLICED

1   In small bowl, with fork, mix soy sauce, vinegar, ginger, and garlic.
2   In 12-inch skillet, toss bok choy and carrots. Fold thin ends of scrod fillets under to create even thickness. Place scrod on top of vegetables. Pour soy-sauce mixture over scrod and sprinkle with green onions; cover and heat to boiling over high heat. Reduce heat to medium; cook until scrod is just opaque throughout, about 10 minutes.

EACH SERVING: ABOUT 200 CALORIES | 34G PROTEIN | 12G CARBOHYDRATE | 2G TOTAL FAT (0G SATURATED) | 3G FIBER | 73MG CHOLESTEROL | 820MG SODIUM ☻ ☺

GINGER-SHALLOT COD ON WATERCRESS

The tangy sauce for this low-fat roasted cod dish features fresh ginger, soy sauce, vinegar, shallot, and hot sauce. Sweet summer squash and spicy watercress round out the meal.

ACTIVE TIME: 25 MINUTES · **TOTAL TIME:** 35 MINUTES
MAKES: 4 MAIN-DISH SERVINGS

1 LARGE SHALLOT, FINELY CHOPPED	⅛ TEASPOON SALT
2 TEASPOONS MINCED, PEELED FRESH GINGER	⅛ TEASPOON FRESHLY GROUND BLACK PEPPER
1 TABLESPOON SHERRY VINEGAR	1 TEASPOON VEGETABLE OIL
4 DROPS HOT-PEPPER SAUCE, SUCH AS TABASCO	2 MEDIUM YELLOW SUMMER SQUASH, THINLY SLICED
3 TABLESPOONS REDUCED-SODIUM SOY SAUCE	12 OUNCES WATERCRESS
1 TABLESPOON BUTTER OR MARGARINE	¼ CUP PACKED FRESH FLAT-LEAF PARSLEY LEAVES, PLUS MORE FOR GARNISH
4 PIECES (4 OUNCES EACH) SKINLESS COD FILLET	

1 Preheat oven to 450°F. Line jelly-roll pan with foil.

2 In 1-quart saucepan, heat shallot, ginger, vinegar, hot sauce, and 2 table-spoons soy sauce to boiling on high heat. Reduce heat to maintain steady simmer; cook 3 to 4 minutes or until liquid is almost evaporated, stirring. Stir in butter; keep sauce warm on low heat.

3 Meanwhile, place cod in prepared pan; sprinkle with salt and pepper. Roast 8 to 10 minutes or until fish just turns opaque throughout. (Instant-read thermometer inserted horizontally into center should register 145°F.)

4 While cod cooks, in 12-inch skillet, heat oil on medium-high heat. Add squash; cook 2 to 3 minutes or until just browned, stirring. Add half of watercress; gently turn to wilt, then add parsley and remaining watercress and 1 tablespoon soy sauce. Cook 1 to 2 minutes or until greens wilt, stir-ring. Transfer to four plates.

5 Arrange cod on top of greens; spoon sauce over fish. Garnish with parsley.

EACH SERVING: ABOUT 160 CALORIES | 22G PROTEIN | 7G CARBOHYDRATE | 5G TOTAL FAT (1G SATURATED) | 2G FIBER | 43MG CHOLESTEROL | 655MG SODIUM ☺

ASIAN FLOUNDER BAKE

Flounder or sole fillets are baked with a luscious gingery sauce. The addition of baby spinach and shredded carrots makes a complete meal.

ACTIVE TIME: 5 MINUTES · **TOTAL TIME:** 20 MINUTES
MAKES: 4 MAIN-DISH SERVINGS

¼ CUP REDUCED-SODIUM SOY SAUCE

2 TABLESPOONS DRY SHERRY

1 TEASPOON GRATED PEELED FRESH GINGER

1 TEASPOON ASIAN SESAME OIL

1 BAG (10 OUNCES) SHREDDED CARROTS

1 BAG (5 TO 6 OUNCES) BABY SPINACH

4 FLOUNDER OR SOLE FILLETS (5 OUNCES EACH)

1 GREEN ONION, THINLY SLICED

1 TABLESPOON SESAME SEEDS, TOASTED (OPTIONAL)

1 Preheat oven to 450°F. In 1-cup liquid measuring cup, combine soy sauce, sherry, sugar, ginger, and sesame oil.

2 In bottom of 13" by 9" baking dish, spread shredded carrots evenly. Place spinach over carrots, then top with flounder. Pour soy-sauce mixture evenly over flounder.

3 Bake until fish turns opaque throughout, 12 to 14 minutes. To serve, sprinkle with green onion and top with sesame seeds, if using.

EACH SERVING: ABOUT 200 CALORIES | 30G PROTEIN | 10G CARBOHYDRATE | 3G TOTAL FAT (1G SATURATED) | 6G FIBER | 68MG CHOLESTEROL | 735MG SODIUM

SEARED SALMON WITH SWEET POTATOES

Simple salmon and sweet potatoes become a gourmet meal in minutes when topped with an easy, tangy lemon-caper sauce and spiked with a hit of spicy cayenne.

ACTIVE TIME: 15 MINUTES · **TOTAL TIME:** 30 MINUTES
MAKES: 4 MAIN-DISH SERVINGS

1   POUND SWEET POTATOES, PEELED AND CUT INTO ½-INCH CUBES

¼   CUP WATER

⅜   TEASPOON SALT

¼   TEASPOON FRESHLY GROUND BLACK PEPPER

1   BAG (6 OUNCES) BABY SPINACH

⅛   TEASPOON CAYENNE (GROUND RED) PEPPER

4   PIECES SKINLESS CENTER-CUT SALMON FILLET (5 OUNCES EACH)

1   LEMON

1   CUP DRY WHITE WINE

2   TEASPOONS CAPERS, RINSED

¼   CUP CHOPPED FRESH FLAT-LEAF PARSLEY

1   In large microwave-safe bowl, combine potatoes, water, and ¼ teaspoon each salt and black pepper. Cover with vented plastic wrap; microwave on High 9 minutes or until tender, stirring halfway through. Add spinach; cover again and microwave 2 minutes longer.

2   Meanwhile, sprinkle cayenne and remaining ⅛ teaspoon salt on salmon. In 12-inch nonstick skillet on medium heat, cook salmon 10 minutes or until knife pierces center easily, turning over halfway through. (Instant-read thermometer inserted horizontally into center of salmon should register 145°F.) Transfer to plate. From lemon, finely grate ½ teaspoon peel onto fish; into cup, squeeze 1 tablespoon juice.

3   To skillet, add wine and capers. Boil on high heat 2 minutes or until liquid is reduced by half, scraping browned bits from pan. Remove from heat; stir in lemon juice and parsley.

4   Divide potato-spinach mixture among plates; top with fish. Spoon wine sauce over fish.

EACH SERVING: ABOUT 300 CALORIES | 31G PROTEIN | 22G CARBOHYDRATE | 9G TOTAL FAT (1G SATURATED) | 4G FIBER | 78MG CHOLESTEROL | 430MG SODIUM ♥ ☺ ♥

SALMON WITH TOMATO-OLIVE RELISH

Lightly season thick salmon steaks with herbes de Provence, a mix of dried herbs—often lavender, basil, thyme, and sage—that originated in southern France. Our tomato and green olive relish adds a burst of bright color and fresh flavor.

ACTIVE TIME: 25 MINUTES · **TOTAL TIME:** 35 MINUTES
MAKES: 4 MAIN-DISH SERVINGS

1 LEMON	2 TEASPOONS HERBES DE PROVENCE
½ CUP GREEN OLIVES, PITTED AND COARSELY CHOPPED	1 TEASPOON FRESHLY GRATED ORANGE PEEL
1 RIPE TOMATO (6 TO 8 OUNCES), CUT INTO ¼-INCH CHUNKS	¾ TEASPOON SALT
1 TABLESPOON MINCED RED ONION	4 SALMON STEAKS, ¾ INCH THICK (6 OUNCES EACH)
1 TABLESPOON FENNEL SEEDS, CRUSHED	

1 From lemon, grate ½ teaspoon peel and squeeze 1 tablespoon juice. In medium bowl, toss lemon peel and juice with olives, tomato, and onion. Cover and refrigerate relish up to 1 day if not serving right away. Makes about 1¼ cups.

2 Prepare outdoor grill for direct grilling over medium heat.

3 In cup, mix fennel seeds, herbes de Provence, orange peel, and salt. Rub herb mixture on both sides of salmon.

4 Place salmon on hot grill rack. Cover and grill until just opaque throughout, about 8 minutes, turning once. (Instant-read thermometer inserted horizontally into salmon should register 145°F.) Serve salmon with relish.

EACH SERVING SALMON WITH ¼ CUP RELISH: ABOUT 295 CALORIES | 29G PROTEIN | 4G CARBOHYDRATE | 18G TOTAL FAT (3G SATURATED) | 2G FIBER | 80MG CHOLESTEROL | 845MG SODIUM ☺

SALMON TERIYAKI

Here's an easy but tasty dish for busy weeknights or a relaxed party with friends. Prepare it in a grill pan or on the outdoor grill. Either way, you can grill up a mix of summer squash and zucchini slices to serve alongside. Just 5 grams of carbs buys you 1 cup sliced squash.

ACTIVE TIME: 10 MINUTES · **TOTAL TIME:** 20 MINUTES
MAKES: 4 MAIN-DISH SERVINGS

6 TABLESPOONS SUGAR-FREE TERIYAKI SAUCE (SEE TIP, PAGE 45)

1 TEASPOON ASIAN SESAME OIL, PLUS ADDITIONAL OIL FOR BRUSHING

4 SALMON STEAKS, ¾ INCH THICK (6 OUNCES EACH)

1 GREEN ONION, THINLY SLICED ON THE DIAGONAL

1 Prepare outdoor grill for direct grilling over medium heat, or preheat a large ridged grill pan to medium.

2 Meanwhile, in 2-quart saucepan, place teriyaki sauce and sesame oil and heat to boiling over medium-high heat. Boil until slightly thickened, 3 minutes, whisking to combine.

3 Lightly brush salmon with oil; place on hot grill rack or pan. Cover and grill, turning over once and brushing frequently with teriyaki mixture, 8 minutes, until salmon just turns opaque throughout. (Instant-read thermometer inserted horizontally into salmon should register 145°F.)

EACH SERVING: ABOUT 310 CALORIES | 36G PROTEIN | 7G CARBOHYDRATE | 15G TOTAL FAT (3G SATURATED) | 0G FIBER | 110MG CHOLESTEROL | 1,120MG SODIUM

ROAST SALMON WITH CAPERS

This whole salmon fillet with a crumb-and-herb topping looks festive, tastes fabulous, and is surprisingly quick and easy to prepare. Serve with a side of lemon broccoli: Steam 2 bags (12 ounces each) precut broccoli florets until tender-crisp, then toss them with 1 tablespoon butter plus 1 tablespoon lemon juice and 1 teaspoon lemon zest; season with salt and pepper to taste. Recipe yields six side-dish servings containing just 5 grams of carbs each.

ACTIVE TIME: 10 MINUTES · TOTAL TIME: 40 MINUTES
MAKES: 6 MAIN-DISH SERVINGS

---

3 TABLESPOONS BUTTER OR MARGARINE	2 TEASPOONS FRESHLY GRATED LEMON PEEL
⅓ CUP PLAIN DRIED BREAD CRUMBS	¼ TEASPOON SALT
¼ CUP LOOSELY PACKED FRESH PARSLEY LEAVES, MINCED	¼ TEASPOON COARSELY GROUND BLACK PEPPER
3 TABLESPOONS DRAINED CAPERS, MINCED	1 WHOLE SALMON FILLET (2 POUNDS)
1 TEASPOON DRIED TARRAGON	LEMON WEDGES FOR GARNISH

1 Preheat oven to 450°F. Line jelly-roll pan with foil; grease foil.

2 In 1-quart saucepan, melt butter over low heat. Remove saucepan from heat; stir in bread crumbs, parsley, capers, tarragon, lemon peel, salt, and pepper.

3 Place salmon, skin side down, in prepared pan. Pat crumb mixture on top. Roast until salmon turns opaque throughout and topping is lightly browned, about 30 minutes. (Instant-read thermometer inserted horizontally into thickest part of fillet should register 145°F.)

4 With two large spatulas, carefully transfer salmon to platter (it's okay if salmon skin sticks to foil). Serve with lemon wedges.

EACH SERVING: ABOUT 325 CALORIES | 28G PROTEIN | 5G CARBOHYDRATE | 21G TOTAL FAT (4G SATURATED) | 0G FIBER | 76MG CHOLESTEROL | 425MG SODIUM ♥

GRILLED TUNA ON SPINACH SALAD

A blend of aromatic spices rubbed on tuna steaks before pan-grilling adds great flavor. A bed of spinach salad tossed with refreshing cucumbers and peppery radishes rounds out the meal.

ACTIVE TIME: 25 MINUTES · **TOTAL TIME:** 35 MINUTES
MAKES: 4 MAIN-DISH SERVINGS

TUNA WITH SPICE RUB

- 1 TABLESPOON OLIVE OIL
- 1 TEASPOON GROUND CUMIN
- 1 TEASPOON GROUND CORIANDER
- 1 TEASPOON PAPRIKA
- 1 TEASPOON FRESHLY GRATED LIME PEEL
- ¾ TEASPOON SALT
- ½ TEASPOON COARSELY GROUND BLACK PEPPER
- 4 TUNA OR SALMON STEAKS, 1 INCH THICK (6 OUNCES EACH)

SPINACH SALAD

- 2 TABLESPOONS OLIVE OIL
- 2 TABLESPOONS FRESH LIME JUICE
- 1 TEASPOON SUGAR
- ¼ TEASPOON GROUND CUMIN
- ¼ TEASPOON SALT
- ⅛ TEASPOON COARSELY GROUND BLACK PEPPER
- 1 BAG (6 OUNCES) BABY SPINACH
- ½ ENGLISH (SEEDLESS) CUCUMBER (8 OUNCES), NOT PEELED, CUT LENGTHWISE IN HALF, THEN THINLY SLICED CROSSWISE
- 1 BUNCH RADISHES, EACH CUT IN HALF, THEN THINLY SLICED

1 Prepare spice rub: In small bowl, with spoon, combine oil, cumin, coriander, paprika, lime peel, salt, and pepper until well blended.

2 Rub spice mixture on both sides of tuna. Heat grill pan over medium heat until hot but not smoking. Add tuna steaks to pan and cook, until tuna just turns opaque throughout, 8 to 10 minutes, turning over once. (Instant-read thermometer inserted horizontally into tuna should register 145°F.) Transfer tuna to cutting board.

3 Meanwhile, prepare spinach salad: In large bowl, with wire whisk, mix oil, lime juice, sugar, cumin, salt, and pepper until dressing is blended. Add spinach, cucumber, and sliced radishes; toss to coat.

4 Cut fish into ½-inch-thick slices. Arrange salad on four dinner plates or large platter; top with fish.

EACH SERVING: ABOUT 300 CALORIES | 42G PROTEIN | 5G CARBOHYDRATE | 12G TOTAL FAT (2G SATURATED) | 5G FIBER | 76MG CHOLESTEROL | 700MG SODIUM ☺

SALMON STEAKS WITH NECTARINE SALAD

The salty-sweet pairing of spice-rubbed salmon and nectarine salad will have your mouth saying more please!

ACTIVE TIME: 20 MINUTES · **TOTAL TIME:** 30 MINUTES

MAKES: 4 MAIN-DISH SERVINGS

2   TEASPOONS VEGETABLE OIL

1   TEASPOON GROUND CORIANDER

1½ TEASPOONS FRESH THYME LEAVES

1¼ TEASPOONS SALT

¼   TEASPOON COARSELY GROUND BLACK PEPPER

4   SALMON STEAKS, ¾ INCH THICK (6 OUNCES EACH)

3   RIPE NECTARINES, PITTED, EACH CUT INTO QUARTERS AND THINLY SLICED CROSSWISE

2   KIRBY CUCUMBERS (4 OUNCES EACH), EACH CUT LENGTHWISE IN HALF, THEN THINLY SLICED CROSSWISE

1   GREEN ONION, THINLY SLICED

1   TABLESPOON FRESH LEMON JUICE

1   Prepare grill for direct grilling over medium heat.

2   Meanwhile, in cup, whisk together oil, coriander, 1 teaspoon thyme, ¾ teaspoon salt, and ⅛ teaspoon pepper. Rub spice mixture on both sides of salmon steaks.

3   In medium bowl, stir nectarines, cucumbers, green onion, lemon juice, and remaining ½ teaspoon thyme, ½ teaspoon salt, and ⅛ teaspoon pepper. Makes about 4½ cups.

4   Lightly grease grill rack. Place salmon on hot rack. Cover grill and cook salmon about 8 minutes or until it just turns opaque throughout, turning over once. (Instant-read thermometer inserted horizontally into salmon should register 145°F.) Serve with nectarine salad.

EACH SERVING: ABOUT 345 CALORIES | 29G PROTEIN | 15G CARBOHYDRATE | 18G TOTAL FAT (3G SATURATED) | 2G FIBER | 80MG CHOLESTEROL | 800MG SODIUM ♥ ☺

MEDITERRANEAN SWORDFISH SALAD

This salad is a deliciously different combination of bold flavors and contrasting textures, with crisp cucumber, juicy grape tomatoes, salty feta cheese, and the meaty grilled goodness of swordfish. Low-carb eating never tasted so good!

ACTIVE TIME: 15 MINUTES · **TOTAL TIME:** 25 MINUTES

MAKES: 4 MAIN-DISH SERVINGS

3   TABLESPOONS OLIVE OIL

1   SWORDFISH STEAK, 1 INCH THICK (1¼ POUNDS)

¼   TEASPOON GROUND BLACK PEPPER

¾   TEASPOON SALT

2   TABLESPOONS FRESH LEMON JUICE

1½ TEASPOONS FRESH OREGANO LEAVES, CHOPPED, OR ½ TEASPOON DRIED OREGANO

1   ENGLISH (SEEDLESS) CUCUMBER, NOT PEELED, CUT INTO ½-INCH CHUNKS

1   PINT GRAPE OR CHERRY TOMATOES, CUT IN HALF

⅓   CUP CRUMBLED FETA CHEESE

1   In 10-inch skillet, heat 1 tablespoon oil over medium-high heat until very hot. Pat swordfish dry with paper towels. Add swordfish to skillet, sprinkle with pepper and ½ teaspoon salt, and cook 10 to 12 minutes or until swordfish is browned on both sides and just opaque throughout, turning over once. (Instant-read thermometer inserted horizontally into center of fish should register 145°F.)

2   Meanwhile, in large bowl, combine lemon juice, oregano, and remaining 2 tablespoons oil and ¼ teaspoon salt.

3   When swordfish is done, transfer to cutting board; trim and discard skin. Cut into 1-inch cubes. Add swordfish, cucumber, and tomatoes to dressing in bowl; toss gently to coat. Sprinkle with feta to serve.

EACH SERVING: ABOUT 315 CALORIES | 32G PROTEIN | 8G CARBOHYDRATE | 17G TOTAL FAT (5G SATURATED) | 2G FIBER | 68MG CHOLESTEROL | 720MG SODIUM 🖤 ☺

SHRIMP AND TOMATO SUMMER SALAD

Want to enjoy this light but satisfying salad year-round? Substitute in plum tomatoes or use 1½ pints cherry tomatoes. For photo, see page 98.

TOTAL TIME: 25 MINUTES

MAKES: 6 MAIN-DISH SERVINGS

2 TABLESPOONS OLIVE OIL	2½ POUNDS RIPE TOMATOES, CUT INTO 1-INCH PIECES
2 TABLESPOONS RED WINE VINEGAR	1 ENGLISH (SEEDLESS) CUCUMBER, CUT LENGTHWISE INTO QUARTERS, THEN CROSSWISE INTO 1-INCH PIECES
¾ TEASPOON SALT	
¼ TEASPOON COARSELY GROUND BLACK PEPPER	1 SMALL RED ONION, CHOPPED
½ CUP LOOSELY PACKED FRESH PARSLEY LEAVES, CHOPPED	2 OUNCES FETA CHEESE, CRUMBLED (½ CUP)
¼ CUP LOOSELY PACKED FRESH MINT LEAVES, THINLY SLICED	
1 POUND SHELLED AND DEVEINED COOKED LARGE SHRIMP (SEE BOX)	

---

1 In serving bowl, with wire whisk, whisk together oil, vinegar, salt, and pepper; stir in parsley and mint.

2 Add shrimp, tomatoes, cucumber, and onion to dressing in bowl; stir to combine. Sprinkle salad with feta. Serve at room temperature, or cover and refrigerate to serve later.

EACH SERVING: ABOUT 200 CALORIES | 20G PROTEIN | 13G CARBOHYDRATE | 8G TOTAL FAT (2G SATURATED) | 3G FIBER | 156MG CHOLESTEROL | 585MG SODIUM ♥ ☺ ≣

SHELLING AND DEVEINING SHRIMP

1 With kitchen shears or a small knife, cut the shrimp shell along the outer curve, just deep enough to expose the dark vein.

2 Working from the cut, gently peel the shell off the shrimp. Discard the shell (or use it to make stock).

3 Hold the shrimp under cold running water; remove the vein with the tip of the knife.

DILLED TUNA-STUFFED TOMATOES

Here's a feast for the eyes and the palate: Slice tomatoes into pretty blossom shapes then stuff each one with a fancy tuna salad featuring bright dill and briney capers. You won't miss the fat, and the tuna mixture retains its creamy consistency. A simple green salad tossed with lemon juice and olive oil is really all you need to complete this fresh and colorful meal.

TOTAL TIME: 25 MINUTES

MAKES: 4 MAIN-DISH SERVINGS

2   KIRBY CUCUMBERS, UNPEELED AND CUT INTO ¼-INCH PIECES

¼   CUP LOOSELY PACKED FRESH DILL, FINELY CHOPPED

¼   CUP SUGAR-FREE LIGHT MAYONNAISE (SEE TIP)

2   TABLESPOONS CAPERS, FINELY CHOPPED

2   TABLESPOONS FRESH LEMON JUICE

1   TABLESPOON DIJON MUSTARD

¼   TEASPOON GROUND BLACK PEPPER

2   CANS (6 OUNCES EACH) SOLID WHITE TUNA IN WATER, DRAINED

4   RIPE LARGE TOMATOES (12 OUNCES EACH)

1   In medium bowl, combine cucumbers, dill, mayonnaise, capers, lemon juice, mustard, pepper, and tuna, flaking tuna with a fork.

2   Cut each tomato, from blossom end, into 6 attached wedges, being careful not to cut all the way through. (Each tomato will form a flower-like shape.) Spoon one-fourth of tuna mixture into center of each tomato.

TIP   Kirkland Signature Real Mayonnaise delivers great taste without any added sugar. If you're watching your fat intake, Walden Farms Miracle Mayo is sugar- and fat-free. Both are available online.

EACH SERVING: ABOUT 255 CALORIES | 18G PROTEIN | 14G CARBOHYDRATE | 14G TOTAL FAT (2G SATURATED) | 3G FIBER | 38MG CHOLESTEROL | 515MG SODIUM ♥ ☺

CRAB COBB SALAD

This lightened version of the traditional Cobb salad features lump crabmeat and a luscious but low-cal yogurt dressing.

TOTAL TIME: 30 MINUTES

MAKES: 4 MAIN-DISH SERVINGS

3   SLICES CENTER-CUT BACON

1   CUP PLAIN LOW-FAT YOGURT

¼   CUP LOOSELY PACKED SNIPPED FRESH CHIVES

1   TABLESPOON DIJON MUSTARD

¼   TEASPOON SALT

¼   TEASPOON FRESHLY GROUND BLACK PEPPER

2   ROMAINE HEARTS, TORN

8   OUNCES LUMP CRABMEAT, PICKED OVER

2   LARGE TOMATOES, SEEDED AND CHOPPED (SEE BOX, OPPOSITE)

1   RIPE AVOCADO, SEEDED AND CHOPPED (SEE BOX, OPPOSITE)

1   On microwave-safe plate, between paper towels, arrange bacon in single layer. Microwave on High 3 minutes or until crisp. When cool, crumble.

2   In a small bowl, with wire whisk, stir yogurt, chives, Dijon, salt, and pepper until well combined.

3   In a large bowl, toss romaine with half of dressing. In small bowl, gently stir half of remaining dressing into crabmeat.

4   Divide romaine among 4 serving plates. Arrange tomatoes, avocado, bacon, and crabmeat in rows over romaine. Spoon remaining dressing over salads and serve.

EACH SERVING: ABOUT 200 CALORIES | 18G PROTEIN | 15G CARBOHYDRATE | 8G TOTAL FAT (2G SATURATED) | 5G FIBER | 64MG CHOLESTEROL | 615MG SODIUM 🔽 ☺

SPEEDY SEED REMOVAL

Seeding and chopping tomatoes and avocados doesn't have to be a slippery business. Just follow these tips and you'll be surprised how easy it can be.

Tomato: Halve tomato and gently dig out the seeds with your fingers. Or cut it into quarters, and use a paring knife to slice out the pulp and seeds using a scooping motion; in this method, you'll lose more flesh, but you're also sure to get all the seeds. Chop tomato as recipe directs.

Avocado: Cut avocado lengthwise in half, cutting around the seed. Twist the two halves to separate them. To remove the seed, give it a whack with the blade of the knife so it is slightly embedded in the seed; cup the avocado in your hand as you twist and lift the seed out. With your fingers, gently peel away the skin from the avocado and discard. Slice or chop the avocado as recipe directs (see Tip).

TIP Avocado flesh darkens quickly when exposed to air; toss with lemon or lime juice to discourage discoloration, or press plastic wrap onto the cut surfaces.

CAJUN SHRIMP WITH RÉMOULADE SAUCE

This down-home dish takes only four minutes on the fire. The creamy homemade sauce (made with light mayonnaise) is the perfect dipper. For a satisfying side, add a colorful slaw of red cabbage and celery.

ACTIVE TIME: 25 MINUTES · **TOTAL TIME:** 30 MINUTES

MAKES: 4 MAIN-DISH SERVINGS

RÉMOULADE SAUCE

- ½ CUP SUGAR-FREE LIGHT MAYONNAISE (SEE TIP, PAGE 121)
- 2 TABLESPOONS SUGAR-FREE KETCHUP (SEE TIP, PAGE 38)
- 2 TABLESPOONS MINCED CELERY
- 1 TABLESPOON GRAINY DIJON MUSTARD
- 1 TABLESPOON MINCED FRESH PARSLEY LEAVES
- 2 TEASPOONS FRESH LEMON JUICE
- ⅓ TEASPOON CAJUN SEASONING
- 1 GREEN ONION, MINCED

CAJUN SHRIMP

- 1 TABLESPOON CAJUN SEASONING
- 1 TABLESPOON OLIVE OIL
- 2 TEASPOONS GRATED FRESH LEMON PEEL PLUS SLIVERED LEMON PEEL FOR GARNISH
- 1¼ POUNDS LARGE SHRIMP, SHELLED AND DEVEINED (SEE BOX, PAGE 120), WITH TAIL PART LEFT ON IF YOU LIKE
- 1 GREEN ONION, CUT INTO SLIVERS FOR GARNISH

LEMON WEDGES (OPTIONAL)

1 Prepare sauce: In small bowl, combine mayonnaise, ketchup, celery, mustard, parsley, lemon juice, Cajun seasoning, and green onion. Cover and refrigerate up to 3 days if not serving right away. Makes about 1 cup.

2 Prepare outdoor grill for direct grilling over medium-high heat. If desired, place flat grill topper on grill to preheat.

3 Prepare shrimp: In medium bowl, mix Cajun seasoning, oil, and grated lemon peel. Add shrimp to bowl and toss until evenly coated.

4 Place shrimp on hot grill rack or grill topper and cook 3 to 4 minutes or until just opaque throughout, turning shrimp over once.

5 Transfer shrimp to platter; garnish with green onion and lemon peel slivers. Serve with rémoulade sauce and, if you like, lemon wedges.

EACH SERVING WITH 2 TABLESPOONS SAUCE: ABOUT 215 CALORIES | 24G PROTEIN | 6G CARBOHYDRATE | 11G TOTAL FAT (3G SATURATED) | 0G FIBER | 181MG CHOLESTEROL | 765MG SODIUM 💚 ☺

SHRIMP ÉTOUFFÉ

Étouffé means "smothered" in Cajun French, and that's just what these shrimp are—smothered in a seasoned tomato sauce that's loaded with flavor. To keep the carbs in check, we've skipped the traditional rice.

ACTIVE TIME: 20 MINUTES · **TOTAL TIME:** 45 MINUTES

MAKES: 4 MAIN-DISH SERVINGS

1	TABLESPOON BUTTER OR MARGARINE	¾	TEASPOON CHILI POWDER
2	TABLESPOONS ALL-PURPOSE FLOUR	½	TEASPOON SALT
1	RED PEPPER, CHOPPED	¼	TEASPOON DRIED THYME
1	LARGE ONION (12 OUNCES), CHOPPED	¼	TEASPOON CAYENNE (GROUND RED) PEPPER
2	CELERY STALKS, THINLY SLICED	½	CUP WATER
2	GARLIC CLOVES, CRUSHED WITH GARLIC PRESS	1	POUND LARGE SHRIMP, SHELLED AND DEVEINED (SEE BOX, PAGE 120)
1	BOTTLE (8 OUNCES) CLAM JUICE	3	GREEN ONIONS, THINLY SLICED
2	TABLESPOONS TOMATO PASTE	½	CUP LOOSELY PACKED FRESH PARSLEY LEAVES, CHOPPED
1	BAY LEAF		

1 In nonstick 12-inch skillet, melt butter over medium heat. Stir in flour and cook, stirring frequently, until golden brown, 4 minutes. Add red pepper, onion, celery, and garlic and cook, stirring occasionally, 5 minutes.

2 Stir in clam juice, tomato paste, bay leaf, chili powder, salt, thyme, cayenne pepper, and water. Heat to boiling over medium heat. Reduce heat to medium-low and simmer, covered, until vegetables are tender, 25 minutes.

3 Add shrimp, green onions, and parsley; simmer, covered, until shrimp turn opaque throughout, about 8 minutes.

EACH SERVING: ABOUT 210 CALORIES | 26G PROTEIN | 16G CARBOHYDRATE | 5G TOTAL FAT (3G SATURATED) | 3G FIBER | 180MG CHOLESTEROL | 684MG SODIUM ☺

MUSSELS WITH CAPERS AND WHITE WINE

Here, we steam shellfish with garlic, capers, and wine. Consider pairing with 1 bunch leeks (1½ pounds) braised in 1 tablespoon butter. It's an elegant dinner that's ready in minutes—and comes in at less than 20 grams of carbs per serving.

ACTIVE TIME: 15 MINUTES · **TOTAL TIME:** 25 MINUTES
MAKES: 4 MAIN-DISH SERVINGS

1 TABLESPOON BUTTER OR MARGARINE	2 TABLESPOONS DRAINED CAPERS
2 TABLESPOONS FINELY CHOPPED SHALLOT	3 POUNDS MUSSELS, SCRUBBED AND DEBEARDED
2 GARLIC CLOVES, CRUSHED WITH GARLIC PRESS	½ CUP LOOSELY PACKED FRESH PARSLEY LEAVES, CHOPPED, FOR GARNISH
½ CUP DRY WHITE WINE	

1 In 5- to 6-quart saucepot or Dutch oven, melt butter over medium-high heat. Add shallot and garlic and cook, stirring frequently, 2 minutes. Stir in wine and capers and heat to boiling; boil 2 minutes.

2 Add mussels to saucepot; reduce heat. Cover and simmer 10 minutes until shells open, transferring mussels to bowl as they open. Discard any mussels that have not opened.

3 Serve mussels in bowls with sauce. Sprinkle with parsley.

EACH SERVING: ABOUT 200 CALORIES | 21G PROTEIN | 9G CARBOHYDRATE | 7G TOTAL FAT (3G SATURATED) | 0G FIBER | 55MG CHOLESTEROL | 650MG SODIUM ♥ ☺

VEGGIES, EGGS & CHEESE

Eggs with vegetables and cheese make terrific low-carb meals. (Check out the "Nutritional Benefits of Eggs" on page 145.) Our egg salads, scrambles, frittatas, and more are perfect for any meal. Or dig into one of our meatless mains: They'll help ensure you eat the recommended five servings of veggies each and every day.

KEY TO ICONS

⊘ 30 minutes or less   ☺ Low calorie   ♥ Heart healthy   🍲 Make ahead   🍲 Slow cooker

Lox Scrambled Eggs (page 142)

ROASTED EGGPLANT PARMESAN

Our skinnier version of eggplant Parm is roasted instead of fried, yet still rich and satisfying. A side salad of arugula and shaved fennel would be a refreshing addition to the meal.

ACTIVE TIME: 35 MINUTES · **TOTAL TIME:** 1 HOUR 20 MINUTES PLUS STANDING
MAKES: 6 MAIN-DISH SERVINGS

- 2 SMALL EGGPLANTS (1¼ POUNDS EACH), CUT INTO ½-INCH-THICK SLICES
- ¼ CUP OLIVE OIL
- ½ TEASPOON SALT
- 1 CAN (28 OUNCES) PLUM TOMATOES, DRAINED AND CHOPPED
- ¼ TEASPOON GROUND BLACK PEPPER
- ⅓ CUP CHOPPED FRESH PARSLEY
- 4 OUNCES MOZZARELLA CHEESE, SHREDDED (1 CUP)
- ½ CUP FRESHLY GRATED PARMESAN CHEESE

1 Preheat oven to 450°F. Place eggplants on two large baking sheets. Brush oil on both sides of eggplant and sprinkle with ¼ teaspoon salt. Roast 15 minutes; turn slices over and roast until eggplant is tender and browned, 20 to 25 minutes.

2 Meanwhile, in nonstick 12-inch skillet, combine tomatoes, remaining ¼ teaspoon salt, and pepper; cook over low heat, stirring occasionally, until tomatoes have thickened, about 20 minutes. Stir in parsley.

3 Adjust oven control to 400°F. In shallow 2½-quart casserole, layer half of eggplant and top with half of tomato sauce; sprinkle with half of mozzarella. Repeat layers; top with Parmesan.

4 Cover loosely with foil and bake casserole until bubbling, about 10 minutes. Remove from oven and let stand at least 10 minutes before serving. Serve hot or at room temperature.

EACH SERVING: ABOUT 250 CALORIES | 11G PROTEIN | 19G CARBOHYDRATE | 16G TOTAL FAT (5G SATURATED) | 6G FIBER | 21MG CHOLESTEROL | 693MG SODIUM ☺

SPINACH ROULADE WITH MUSHROOMS

Spinach gives this roll its attractive green color. To create an even more colorful meal, pair it with 1 pint of ripe cherry tomatoes sautéed in 1 tablespoon butter. Sprinkle with parsley and serve immediately. It makes four side-dish servings at 2 grams of carbs apiece.

ACTIVE TIME: 25 MINUTES · **TOTAL TIME:** 40 MINUTES
MAKES: 8 MAIN-DISH SERVINGS

1 TABLESPOON BUTTER OR MARGARINE	1 PACKAGE (10 OUNCES) FROZEN CHOPPED SPINACH, THAWED AND SQUEEZED DRY
2 GREEN ONIONS, THINLY SLICED	
8 OUNCES WHITE MUSHROOMS, TRIMMED AND COARSELY CHOPPED	6 LARGE EGGS
8 OUNCES SHIITAKE MUSHROOMS, STEMS REMOVED AND CAPS THINLY SLICED	⅔ CUP MILK
	½ CUP FRESHLY GRATED PARMESAN CHEESE
½ TEASPOON SALT	6 OUNCES MILD OR SHARP CHEDDAR CHEESE, SHREDDED (1½ CUPS)
¼ TEASPOON GROUND BLACK PEPPER	

1 Preheat oven to 350°F. Line 15½" by 10½" jelly-roll pan with foil, leaving 2-inch overhang at each short end; grease foil.

2 In nonstick 12-inch skillet, melt butter over medium heat. Add green onions and cook until wilted, about 1 minute. Add white and shiitake mushrooms, salt, and pepper; cook, stirring frequently, until mushrooms are tender and liquid has evaporated, about 7 minutes. Remove from heat.

3 In blender, puree spinach, eggs, milk, and Parmesan until smooth. Pour into prepared pan, smoothing top with rubber spatula. Bake just until spinach mixture is set, 8 to 10 minutes.

4 Lift foil with spinach mixture and place on work surface. Sprinkle with Cheddar and spread mushroom mixture on top. Roll up from one long end, using foil to help roll, and place, seam side down, in jelly-roll pan. Bake until Cheddar melts, about 5 minutes longer. To serve, using serrated knife, cut into 8 thick slices.

EACH SERVING: ABOUT 215 CALORIES | 15G PROTEIN | 6G CARBOHYDRATE | 15G TOTAL FAT (8G SATURATED) | 193MG CHOLESTEROL | 490MG SODIUM ☺

BROCCOLI-CHEESE POLENTA PIZZA

Here's a creative low-carb take on pizza featuring the toothsome corn goodness of ready-made polenta topped with tomatoes, broccoli, and two kinds of cheese.

ACTIVE TIME: 20 MINUTES · **TOTAL TIME:** 25 MINUTES
MAKES: 5 MAIN-DISH SERVINGS

OLIVE OIL NONSTICK COOKING SPRAY

1 LOG (16 OUNCES) PRECOOKED PLAIN POLENTA, CUT INTO ¼-INCH-THICK SLICES

1 BAG (12 OUNCES) BROCCOLI FLORETS

2 TABLESPOONS WATER

¾ CUP PART-SKIM RICOTTA CHEESE

¼ CUP FRESHLY GRATED PARMESAN CHEESE

1 TEASPOON GRATED LEMON PEEL

⅛ TEASPOON GROUND BLACK PEPPER

1 LARGE RIPE PLUM TOMATO, CHOPPED

1 Preheat broiler and place rack about 4 inches from heat source.

2 Coat 12-inch pizza pan or large cookie sheet with cooking spray. In center of pizza pan, place 1 slice polenta; arrange remaining slices in two concentric circles around first slice, overlapping slightly, to form 10-inch round. Generously coat polenta with cooking spray. Broil polenta until heated through, about 5 minutes. Do not turn broiler off.

3 Meanwhile, in microwave-safe medium bowl, combine broccoli and water. Cover with plastic wrap, turning back one section to vent. Heat broccoli in microwave oven on High 3 minutes or just until tender. Drain.

4 In small bowl, combine ricotta, Parmesan, lemon peel, and pepper.

5 Arrange broccoli evenly over polenta. Drop cheese mixture by tablespoons over polenta and broccoli; sprinkle with tomato. Broil pizza until topping is hot, 3 to 5 minutes.

EACH SERVING: ABOUT 160 CALORIES | 10G PROTEIN | 20G CARBOHYDRATE | 5G TOTAL FAT (2G SATURATED) | 3G FIBER | 14MG CHOLESTEROL | 425MG SODIUM ☻ ☺

THAI COCONUT SOUP

Tofu, mixed veggies, fresh ginger, and Asian seasonings make this creamy coconut soup a winner.

ACTIVE TIME: 10 MINUTES · **TOTAL TIME:** 20 MINUTES

MAKES: 9 CUPS OR 4 MAIN-DISH SERVINGS

---

2 SMALL CARROTS, EACH CUT CROSSWISE IN HALF

½ RED PEPPER

1 CAN (14 OUNCES) LIGHT UNSWEETENED COCONUT MILK (NOT CREAM OF COCONUT), WELL STIRRED

2 GARLIC CLOVES, CRUSHED WITH GARLIC PRESS

1 (2-INCH) PIECE PEELED FRESH GINGER, CUT INTO 4 SLICES

½ TEASPOON GROUND CORIANDER

½ TEASPOON GROUND CUMIN

¼ TEASPOON CAYENNE (GROUND RED) PEPPER

12 OUNCES FIRM TOFU, CUT INTO 1-INCH CUBES

2 CANS (14½ OUNCES EACH) VEGETABLE BROTH

1 TABLESPOON SUGAR-FREE ASIAN FISH SAUCE (SEE TIP, PAGE 21)

1 TABLESPOON FRESH LIME JUICE

1 CUP WATER

2 GREEN ONIONS, SLICED

½ CUP CHOPPED FRESH CILANTRO LEAVES

1 With vegetable peeler, slice carrots and red pepper lengthwise into very thin strips. Set aside.

2 In 5-quart Dutch oven, heat ½ cup coconut milk to boiling over medium heat. Add garlic, ginger, coriander, cumin, and cayenne; cook, stirring, 1 minute.

3 Increase heat to medium-high. Stir in carrot strips, pepper strips, tofu, broth, fish sauce, lime juice, water, and remaining coconut milk; heat just to simmering.

4 Discard ginger slices. Stir in green onions and cilantro just before serving.

EACH SERVING: ABOUT 210 CALORIES | 11G PROTEIN | 14G CARBOHYDRATE | 17G TOTAL FAT (6G SATURATED) | 2G FIBER | 0MG CHOLESTEROL | 1,050MG SODIUM ❤ ☺ 🍴

GRILLED TOFU AND VEGGIES

Instead of veggie burgers, grill up this satisfying meatless main. Be sure to use extra-firm tofu; other varieties may fall apart on the grill.

ACTIVE TIME: 25 MINUTES · **TOTAL TIME:** 35 MINUTES

MAKES: 4 MAIN-DISH SERVINGS

HOISIN GLAZE

⅓ CUP SUGAR-FREE HOISIN SAUCE (SEE TIP, PAGE 23)

2 GARLIC CLOVES, CRUSHED WITH GARLIC PRESS

1 TABLESPOON VEGETABLE OIL

1 TABLESPOON REDUCED-SODIUM SOY SAUCE

1 TABLESPOON GRATED, PEELED FRESH GINGER

1 TABLESPOON RICE VINEGAR

⅛ TEASPOON CAYENNE (GROUND RED) PEPPER

TOFU AND VEGGIES

1 PACKAGE (15 OUNCES) EXTRA-FIRM TOFU

2 MEDIUM ZUCCHINI (10 OUNCES EACH), EACH CUT LENGTHWISE INTO QUARTERS, THEN CROSSWISE IN HALF

1 LARGE RED PEPPER, CUT LENGTHWISE INTO QUARTERS, STEM AND SEEDS DISCARDED

1 BUNCH GREEN ONIONS, TRIMMED

1 TEASPOON VEGETABLE OIL

1 Prepare hoisin glaze: In small bowl, with fork, mix hoisin, garlic, oil, soy sauce, ginger, vinegar, and cayenne until well blended; set aside.

2 Prepare outdoor grill for direct grilling over medium heat.

3 Prepare tofu and veggies: Cut tofu horizontally into 4 pieces, then cut each piece crosswise in half. Place tofu on paper towels; pat dry with more paper towels. Spoon half of hoisin glaze into medium bowl; add zucchini and red pepper. Gently toss vegetables to coat. Arrange tofu on large plate; brush with remaining glaze. On another plate, rub green onions with oil.

4 Arrange tofu, zucchini, and red pepper on hot grill rack. Grill tofu 6 minutes, gently turning over once with wide metal spatula. Transfer tofu to platter; keep warm. Grill vegetables until warm and tender, about 5 minutes longer, transferring them to platter with tofu as they are done. Add green onions to grill during last minute of cooking time; grill until lightly browned. Transfer to platter and serve hot.

EACH SERVING: ABOUT 210 CALORIES | 15G PROTEIN | 14G CARBOHYDRATE | 11G TOTAL FAT (1G SATURATED) | 4G FIBER | 0MG CHOLESTEROL | 615MG SODIUM ☺

TOMATO TARTE TATIN

Frozen puff pastry is the low-carb secret to this single-skillet dish.

ACTIVE TIME: 30 MINUTES · **TOTAL TIME:** 1 HOUR

MAKES: 8 MAIN-DISH SERVINGS

---

1 FROZEN SHEET PUFF PASTRY (HALF 17.3-OUNCE PACKAGE), THAWED

1 TABLESPOON OLIVE OIL

1 MEDIUM ONION (8 TO 10 OUNCES), CHOPPED

1 LARGE YELLOW PEPPER (8 TO 10 OUNCES), CHOPPED

½ TEASPOON SALT

¼ TEASPOON FRESHLY GROUND BLACK PEPPER

1 TEASPOON CHOPPED FRESH THYME LEAVES

2 TABLESPOONS BUTTER (NO SUBSTITUTIONS)

1½ POUNDS FIRM RIPE PLUM TOMATOES, SEEDED (SEE TIP, PAGE 123), CUT IN HALF LENGTHWISE

3 OUNCES GOAT CHEESE, CRUMBLED

8 SMALL FRESH BASIL LEAVES

1 Preheat oven to 400°F. On lightly floured surface, with floured rolling pin, roll pastry into 12 inch square; cut into 12 inch round. Place on waxed paper–lined cookie sheet; refrigerate.

2 In 12-inch heavy ovenproof skillet, heat oil on medium heat. Add onion, yellow pepper, and ⅛ teaspoon each salt and pepper. Cook 6 minutes or just until tender, stirring. Stir in thyme; cook 1 minute. Transfer to bowl.

3 In same pan, melt butter. Add tomatoes, cut sides down, in single layer; cover, cook 2 minutes, then uncover. Cook 3 to 4 minutes longer or until most of pan juices are reduced and thickened, swirling pan frequently. Turn tomatoes over; sprinkle with ¼ teaspoon salt and remaining ⅛ teaspoon pepper. Cook 2 minutes or until softened and most of liquid has evaporated, swirling pan. (Any remaining liquid should be thick and glossy.)

4 Remove pan from heat. Sprinkle onion mixture over and between tomatoes. Carefully invert dough (still on waxed paper) onto mixture in pan; discard paper. Cut six small slits in top of dough. Bake 30 to 35 minutes or until crust is dark golden brown. Cool in pan on wire rack 10 minutes.

5 To unmold, place platter over top of tart. Quickly and carefully turn platter with skillet upside down to invert tart; remove skillet. Sprinkle tart with remaining ⅛ teaspoon salt, goat cheese, and basil. Serve immediately.

EACH SERVING: ABOUT 210 CALORIES | 5G PROTEIN | 11G CARBOHYDRATE | 14G TOTAL FAT (5G SATURATED) | 2G FIBER | 13MG CHOLESTEROL | 330MG SODIUM ☺ ❤

EGG SALAD DELUXE

Hard-cooked eggs are chopped and mixed with sautéed onions, mushrooms, and celery for a new take on classic egg salad. Serve on sweet, tender Boston lettuce leaves.

ACTIVE TIME: 20 MINUTES · **TOTAL TIME:** 40 MINUTES
MAKES: 4½ CUPS OR 6 MAIN-DISH SERVINGS

8   LARGE EGGS

3   TABLESPOONS OLIVE OIL

1   ONION, CUT IN HALF AND THINLY SLICED

10 OUNCES MUSHROOMS, SLICED

2   STALKS CELERY, FINELY CHOPPED

¼   CUP LOOSELY PACKED FRESH PARSLEY LEAVES, CHOPPED

½   TEASPOON SALT

¼   TEASPOON COARSELY GROUND BLACK PEPPER

1   HEAD BOSTON LETTUCE, LEAVES SEPARATED

1   In 3-quart saucepan, place eggs and enough cold *water* to cover by at least 1 inch; heat to boiling on high heat. Immediately remove saucepan from heat and cover tightly; let stand 15 minutes. Cool eggs under cold running water until easy to handle.

2   Meanwhile, in nonstick 12-inch skillet, heat 1 tablespoon oil over medium heat until hot. Add onion and cook, stirring occasionally, until tender and golden, 10 to 12 minutes. Increase heat to medium-high; add mushrooms and cook until mushrooms are golden and all liquid evaporates, 8 minutes.

3   Remove shells from hard-cooked eggs. Finely chop eggs. In large bowl, toss eggs with mushroom mixture, celery, parsley, salt, pepper, and remaining 2 tablespoons oil.

4   To serve, line platter with lettuce leaves and top with egg salad.

EACH SERVING: ABOUT 190 CALORIES | 11G PROTEIN | 5G CARBOHYDRATE | 14G TOTAL FAT (3G SATURATED) | 1G FIBER | 283MG CHOLESTEROL | 290MG SODIUM 😊 📦

TOFU "EGG SALAD"

The familiar egg-salad seasonings lend themselves well to tofu. For a light lunch, serve with a mini pita bread (6.5 grams carbs), lettuce, and tomato wedges.

TOTAL TIME: 15 MINUTES
MAKES: 4 MAIN-DISH SERVINGS

1 PACKAGE (15 OUNCES) FIRM TOFU, DRAINED	¼ CUP SUGAR-FREE LIGHT MAYONNAISE (SEE TIP, PAGE 121)
1 STALK CELERY, CHOPPED	½ TEASPOON SALT
½ SMALL RED PEPPER, FINELY CHOPPED	⅛ TEASPOON TURMERIC
1 GREEN ONION, CHOPPED	

In medium bowl, with fork, mash tofu until it resembles scrambled eggs; stir in celery, red pepper, green onion, mayonnaise, salt, and turmeric. Cover and refrigerate up to 1 day if not serving right away.

TIP For a vegan version, substitute a nondairy mayonnaise, such as Vegenaise, which is sweetened with a little brown rice syrup.

EACH SERVING: ABOUT 195 CALORIES | 18G PROTEIN | 10G CARBOHYDRATE | 11G TOTAL FAT (1G SATURATED) | 0MG CHOLESTEROL | 455MG SODIUM ● ☺ ♥

SHRIMP EGG SALAD WITH SPRING PEAS

Made without mayo, this company-worthy combo of egg, shrimp, and potato salad gets its creaminess from a tangy yogurt-and-mustard dressing. It's plated alongside fresh snap peas tossed in a light and luscious lemon-dill vinaigrette.

ACTIVE TIME: 1 HOUR 5 MINUTES · TOTAL TIME: 1 HOUR 25 MINUTES
MAKES: 6 MAIN-DISH SERVINGS

---

12 LARGE EGGS

1 LEMON

3 SPRIGS FRESH DILL, LEAVES CHOPPED, STEMS RESERVED

12 OUNCES SHELLED AND DEVEINED LARGE SHRIMP (16 TO 20 COUNT)

6 OUNCES YUKON GOLD POTATOES, SCRUBBED AND CUT INTO ½-INCH CHUNKS

⅞ TEASPOON SALT

12 OUNCES SUGAR SNAP PEAS, STRINGS REMOVED, CUT IN HALVES AT AN ANGLE

1½ CUPS FROZEN PEAS

1 CUP PLAIN YOGURT

1 TABLESPOON DIJON MUSTARD

⅜ TEASPOON FRESHLY GROUND BLACK PEPPER

½ CUP FINELY CHOPPED RED ONION (FROM 1 SMALL ONION)

3 STALKS CELERY, FINELY CHOPPED

1 TABLESPOON WHITE WINE VINEGAR

2 TABLESPOONS OLIVE OIL

1 In 4-quart saucepan, place eggs and enough cold *water* to cover by 1 inch. Heat to boiling on high; remove from heat. Cover and let stand 5 minutes. With slotted spoon, transfer eggs to colander. Rinse eggs under cold water until cool enough to handle; peel and cut in quarters. Set aside 12 quarters for garnish.

2 From lemon, squeeze 3 tablespoons juice and reserve. To same saucepan of water, add lemon rind and dill stems; heat to boiling on high heat. Add shrimp, reduce heat to maintain bare simmer, and cook 3 minutes or until shrimp just turn opaque throughout. Drain, rinse under cold water until cool, and drain again. Discard lemon rind and dill stems.

3 In same pan, place potatoes and enough cold *water* to cover. Add ½ teaspoon salt. Heat to boiling on high heat, cover, and reduce heat to simmer 15 minutes or until just tender; drain well.

4 While potatoes cook, heat 3-quart saucepan of *water* to boiling on high. Add snap peas and frozen peas. Cook 2 minutes or until bright green; drain well.

5 In large bowl, whisk yogurt, mustard, 1 tablespoon lemon juice, and ¼ teaspoon each salt and pepper. Add hot potatoes, onion, celery, shrimp, eggs, and half of chopped dill. Fold gently until well combined.

6 In another large bowl, whisk vinegar, oil, remaining 2 tablespoons lemon juice, and remaining ⅛ teaspoon each salt and pepper; add all peas and remaining dill. Toss until well coated.

7 Spoon shrimp salad into center of serving platter, then spoon pea mixture all around. Garnish with reserved egg quarters and serve immediately.

EACH SERVING: ABOUT 350 CALORIES | 26G PROTEIN | 20G CARBOHYDRATE | 17G TOTAL FAT (5G SATURATED) | 4G FIBER | 450MG CHOLESTEROL | 760MG SODIUM ☺

LOX SCRAMBLED EGGS

For this fast feed-a-crowd dish, just soft-scramble a dozen eggs with savory bagel-shop staples—smoked salmon and cream cheese. Sprinkle with onions and capers and serve family-style with sliced tomatoes. For photo, see page 128.

ACTIVE TIME: 20 MINUTES · **TOTAL TIME:** 25 MINUTES
MAKES: 6 MAIN-DISH SERVINGS

12 LARGE EGGS

2 TABLESPOONS HEAVY CREAM

¼ TEASPOON SALT

1½ TABLESPOONS BUTTER OR MARGARINE

3 TABLESPOONS CREAM CHEESE, CUT UP

4 OUNCES SLICED SMOKED SALMON, FLAKED INTO SMALL PIECES

2 TABLESPOONS FINELY CHOPPED RED ONION

1 TABLESPOON CHOPPED, RINSED CAPERS

1 TABLESPOON CHOPPED FRESH DILL LEAVES

2 POUNDS ASSORTED TOMATOES, SLICED

6 MINI BAGELS, SPLIT AND TOASTED

1 In large bowl, with fork, beat eggs, cream, and salt until well blended.

2 In nonstick 12-inch skillet, melt butter on medium heat. Add egg mixture to skillet and cook, stirring with spatula, until eggs are almost cooked, 6 to 8 minutes. Fold in cream cheese and salmon. Cook 1 minute longer or until egg mixture is set but still moist, stirring.

3 Place eggs on serving platter. Sprinkle onion, capers, and dill over eggs. Garnish with tomatoes and serve with mini bagels.

EACH SERVING: ABOUT 310 CALORIES | 20G PROTEIN | 17G CARBOHYDRATE | 18G TOTAL FAT (7G SATURATED) | 1G FIBER | 391MG CHOLESTEROL | 600MG SODIUM 🟢 ☺

SCRAMBLED EGGS WITH CHIVES

Serve these chive-flecked eggs alongside platters of crispy bacon and grapefruit wedges to feed the whole gang with ease.

ACTIVE TIME: 10 MINUTES · **TOTAL TIME:** 20 MINUTES
MAKES: 12 MAIN-DISH SERVINGS

24 LARGE EGGS

¾ CUP LOW-FAT (1%) MILK

½ CUP SNIPPED FRESH CHIVES
(2 LARGE BUNCHES)

¾ TEASPOON SALT

¼ TEASPOON COARSELY GROUND
BLACK PEPPER

2 TABLESPOONS BUTTER OR
MARGARINE

1 In large bowl, with wire whisk, beat eggs, milk, chives, salt, and pepper until blended.

2 In deep nonstick 12-inch skillet, melt butter over medium heat. Add egg mixture to skillet. As egg mixture begins to set around edges, stir lightly with heat-safe rubber spatula or wooden spoon to allow uncooked egg mixture to flow toward side of pan. Continue cooking until eggs are set to desired doneness, 7 to 10 minutes. Serve immediately.

EACH SERVING: ABOUT 175 CALORIES | 13G PROTEIN | 2G CARBOHYDRATE | 12G TOTAL FAT
(5G SATURATED) | 0G FIBER | 435MG CHOLESTEROL | 296MG SODIUM ♥ ☺

BACON AND EGGS OVER ASPARAGUS

Here's a bistro-style take on classic bacon and eggs served over roasted thyme-scented asparagus. It's a fun twist that will be well-received whether you serve it for brunch or supper.

ACTIVE TIME: 8 MINUTES · **TOTAL TIME:** 30 MINUTES
MAKES: 4 MAIN-DISH SERVINGS

8 SLICES BACON

1 POUND ASPARAGUS SPEARS, TRIMMED

½ TEASPOON FRESH THYME LEAVES, CHOPPED

⅜ TEASPOON GROUND BLACK PEPPER

8 LARGE EGGS

⅛ TEASPOON SALT

3 TABLESPOONS PACKED FRESH FLAT-LEAF PARSLEY LEAVES, CHOPPED

1 TABLESPOON FRESH DILL, CHOPPED

1   Preheat oven to 475°F. In 18" by 12" jelly-roll pan, arrange bacon slices in single layer, spacing ¼ inch apart. Roast 8 to 9 minutes or until browned and crisp. Transfer to paper-towel-lined plate; set aside. Drain and discard excess bacon fat in pan, leaving thin film of fat.

2   Add asparagus to pan in single layer. Roll in fat until evenly coated. Arrange so that bottoms of spears touch one long side of pan. Sprinkle thyme and ¼ teaspoon pepper on asparagus. Roast 8 to 10 minutes or until asparagus spears are tender and browned.

3   Carefully crack eggs, without breaking yolks (see Tip), directly onto asparagus spears, staggering if necessary and spacing ¼ inch apart. Carefully return pan to oven. Roast 5 to 6 minutes or until whites are just set and yolks are still runny. Sprinkle salt and remaining ⅛ teaspoon pepper on eggs. Return bacon to pan; sprinkle eggs and asparagus with parsley and dill. To serve, use wide spatula to transfer to serving plates.

TIP If you're worried about breaking the egg yolks, crack each egg, one at a time, into a small cup or bowl before pouring it onto the asparagus.

EACH SERVING: ABOUT 235 CALORIES | 18G PROTEIN | 4G CARBOHYDRATE | 16G TOTAL FAT (5G SATURATED) | 1G FIBER | 435MG CHOLESTEROL | 405MG SODIUM ♥ ☺

NUTRITIONAL BENEFITS OF EGGS

Eggs got a bum rap for years. Yes, the yolk of an egg does contain cholesterol, but as hundreds of studies can attest, if eaten in moderation, eggs won't raise a person's overall cholesterol level. And eggs have so much to offer nutritionally. A single egg is a good source of selenium, which provides antioxidant protection; iodine, vital to thyroid function; energy-producing B_2; and protein.

EGGS FLORENTINE

This slimmed-down recipe is every bit as satisfying as the calorie-laden classic. Instead of carb-loaded English muffins, we top slices of pre-cooked polenta with Canadian bacon and creamed spinach flavored with grated Parmesan cheese. Serve with a side salad of bitter greens like radicchio and frisée tossed with Italian dressing.

ACTIVE TIME: 25 MINUTES · **TOTAL TIME:** 45 MINUTES
MAKES: 6 MAIN-DISH SERVINGS

---

1   LOG (16 OUNCES) PRECOOKED POLENTA

6   SLICES CANADIAN-STYLE BACON (4 OUNCES)

1½ CUPS LOW-FAT (1%) MILK

1   TABLESPOON CORNSTARCH

½   TEASPOON SALT

PINCH CAYENNE (GROUND RED) PEPPER

½   CUP WATER

1   PACKAGE (10 OUNCES) FROZEN CHOPPED SPINACH, THAWED AND SQUEEZED DRY

¼   CUP GRATED PARMESAN CHEESE

6   LARGE EGGS, COLD

---

1   Preheat oven to 400°F. Grease shallow 2½-quart casserole. Cut polenta log in half, then cut each half lengthwise into 3 long slices. Place polenta slices in single layer in casserole. Bake slices until heated through, 15 minutes. Top each polenta slice with 1 slice bacon; bake 5 minutes longer. Keep warm.

2   Meanwhile, in 2-quart saucepan, with wire whisk, mix milk, cornstarch, salt, cayenne, and water until blended. Cook over medium-high heat until mixture thickens and boils; boil 1 minute, stirring. Stir in spinach and Parmesan; heat through.

3   In 12-inch skillet, heat 1½ *inches water* to boiling over medium-high heat. Reduce heat to medium to maintain gentle simmer. Break 1 egg into cup; holding cup close to surface of water, slip egg in. Repeat with remaining eggs. Poach eggs 3 to 5 minutes. With slotted spoon, lift out each egg; quickly drain in spoon on paper towels.

4   To serve, place 1 bacon-topped polenta slice on each plate. Spoon spinach mixture over bacon and polenta; top with poached egg.

EACH SERVING: ABOUT 215 CALORIES | 16G PROTEIN | 18G CARBOHYDRATE | 8G TOTAL FAT (3G SATURATED) | 2G FIBER | 226MG CHOLESTEROL | 995MG SODIUM ☺

HERB AND FETA FRITTATA

This easy one-dish meal is a great jumping off point for many variations. Experiment with different kinds of cheese, such as grated Gruyère, crumbled goat cheese, or Brie cut into half-inch pieces. If you're a bacon lover, crumble some into the frittata, or serve whole slices on the side.

ACTIVE TIME: 10 MINUTES · **TOTAL TIME:** 30 MINUTES

MAKES: 4 MAIN-DISH SERVINGS

2 TEASPOONS OLIVE OIL

8 LARGE EGGS

4 OUNCES FETA CHEESE, CRUMBLED (1 CUP)

⅓ CUP LOOSELY PACKED FRESH PARSLEY OR BASIL LEAVES, CHOPPED

¼ CUP WHOLE MILK

2 TABLESPOONS FRESH ROSEMARY OR THYME LEAVES, CHOPPED

½ TEASPOON GROUND BLACK PEPPER

1 Preheat oven to 400°F. In nonstick 10-inch skillet with oven-safe handle (if skillet is not oven-safe, wrap handle with double layer of foil), heat oil over medium heat until hot.

2 Meanwhile, in medium bowl with wire whisk, whisk eggs, feta, parsley, milk, rosemary, and pepper until blended. Pour egg mixture into skillet; do not stir. Cook until egg mixture begins to set around edges, 3 to 4 minutes.

3 Place skillet in oven; bake until frittata is set, 13 to 15 minutes. Cut frittata into wedges and serve.

EACH SERVING: ABOUT 255 CALORIES | 17G PROTEIN | 4G CARBOHYDRATE | 19G TOTAL FAT (8G SATURATED) | 0G FIBER | 452MG CHOLESTEROL | 450MG SODIUM ✔ ☺

ASPARAGUS AND GREEN-ONION FRITTATA

Everyone loves a skillet omelet, especially when it's filled with bits of cream cheese and sautéed vegetables. Serve with a garden-fresh tomato salad drizzled with extra-virgin olive oil and sprinkled with chopped fresh basil. One medium tomato contributes just 5 grams of carbs.

ACTIVE TIME: 25 MINUTES · **TOTAL TIME:** 35 MINUTES

MAKES: 4 MAIN-DISH SERVINGS

8	LARGE EGGS	1	TABLESPOON BUTTER OR MARGARINE
½	CUP WHOLE MILK	1	BUNCH GREEN ONIONS, CHOPPED
⅛	TEASPOON GROUND BLACK PEPPER	2	OUNCES NEUFCHÂTEL CHEESE
¾	TEASPOON SALT		
12	OUNCES ASPARAGUS, TRIMMED		

1 Preheat oven to 375°F. In medium bowl, with wire whisk, beat eggs, milk, pepper, and ½ teaspoon salt until blended; set aside. If using thin asparagus, cut each stalk crosswise in half; if using thicker asparagus, cut stalks into 1-inch pieces.

2 In nonstick 10-inch skillet with oven-safe handle, melt butter over medium heat. Add asparagus and remaining ¼ teaspoon salt; cook 4 minutes for thin stalks or 6 minutes for thicker stalks, stirring often. Stir in green onions and cook, stirring occasionally, until vegetables are tender, 2 to 3 minutes longer.

3 Reduce heat to medium-low. Pour egg mixture over vegetables in skillet; drop scant teaspoonfuls of cream cheese on top of egg mixture. Cook, without stirring, until egg mixture begins to set around edge, 3 to 4 minutes. Place skillet in oven and bake until frittata is set, 10 to 12 minutes. Cut into wedges to serve.

EACH SERVING: ABOUT 250 CALORIES | 17G PROTEIN | 6G CARBOHYDRATE | 18G TOTAL FAT (8G SATURATED) | 1G FIBER | 448MG CHOLESTEROL | 689MG SODIUM ☺

GENERAL INDEX

Note: Page numbers in **bold** indicate recipe category summaries/overviews.

INDEX OF RECIPES BY ICON

This index makes it easy to search recipes by category, including 30 minutes or less, heart-healthy, low-calorie, make-ahead, and slow-cooker dishes.

☺ **LOW CALORIE**

This list will come in handy if you're keeping track of your daily caloric intake. Main-dishes meals (which include a starch or fruit) that are 450 calories or less per serving are included, along with all other main dishes that are 300 calories or less per serving.

▦ MAKE AHEAD

For convenience, you can make all (or a portion) of these recipes ahead of time. The individual recipes indicate which steps you can do-ahead or how long you can refrigerate or freeze the completed dish.

▥ SLOW COOKER

These slow-cooked dishes make it easy to get dinner on the table. Just put all the ingredients in the bowl of your slow cooker in the A.M., and you'll have a delicious, ready-to-serve main dish in the P.M.

PHOTOGRAPHY CREDITS

James Baigrie: 2, 59, 89, 98
Corbis: Andrew Scrivani/the food passionates, 91;
Brian Hagiwara: 19, 22, 27, 32, 37, 52, 62, 85, 97, 118, 124
iStockphoto: Mariya Bibikova, 10; Nikola Bilic, 55; clubfoto, 29; Donald Erickson, 13; Tobias Helbig, 25; hudiemm, 109; Liza McCorkle, 12; Giancarlo Polacchini, 105; Frans Rombout, 71; Roberto A. Sanchez, 127; Klaudia Steiner, 87; YinYang, 9
Kate Mathis: 11, 41, 68, 103, 110, 123
Ngoc Minh Ngo: 133
Con Poulos: 42
Alan Richardson: 47, 73, 76, 81, 93, 106, 145, 148
Kate Sears: 14
Shutterstock: Irina Fischer, 48; Smit, 113; Yasonya, 139
Studio D: 51; Philip Friedman, 7; Ylva Erevall, 143
Mark Thomas: 115
Anna Williams: 6, 65, 128, 136, 141

Front Cover: Brian Hagiwara
Spine: iStockphoto/clubfoto
Back Cover: Kate Mathis (top left), Brian Hagiwara (top right, bottom)

METRIC EQUIVALENTS

The recipes that appear in this cookbook use the standard United States method for measuring liquid and dry or solid ingredients (teaspoons, tablespoons, and cups). The information on this chart is provided to help cooks outside the U.S. successfully use these recipes. All equivalents are approximate.

METRIC EQUIVALENTS FOR DIFFERENT TYPES OF INGREDIENTS

A standard cup measure of a dry or solid ingredient will vary in weight depending on the type of ingredient. A standard cup of liquid is the same volume for any type of liquid. Use the following chart when converting standard cup measures to grams (weight) or milliliters (volume).

Standard Cup	Fine Powder *(e.g. flour)*	Grain *(e.g. rice)*	Granular *(e.g. sugar)*	Liquid Solids *(e.g. butter)*	Liquid *(e.g. milk)*
1	140 g	150 g	190 g	200 g	240 ml
¾	105 g	113 g	143 g	150 g	180 ml
⅔	93 g	100 g	125 g	133 g	160 ml
½	70 g	75 g	95 g	100 g	120 ml
⅓	47 g	50 g	63 g	67 g	80 ml
¼	35 g	38 g	48 g	50 g	60 ml
⅛	18 g	19 g	24 g	25 g	30 ml

USEFUL EQUIVALENTS FOR LIQUID INGREDIENTS BY VOLUME

¼ tsp	=							1 ml		
½ tsp	=							2 ml		
1 tsp	=							5 ml		
3 tsp	=	1 tbls	=			½ fl oz	=	15 ml		
		2 tbls	=	⅛ cup	=	1 fl oz	=	30 ml		
		4 tbls	=	¼ cup	=	2 fl oz	=	60 ml		
		5⅓ tbls	=	⅓ cup	=	3 fl oz	=	80 ml		
		8 tbls	=	½ cup	=	4 fl oz	=	120 ml		
		10⅔ tbls	=	⅔ cup	=	5 fl oz	=	160 ml		
		12 tbls	=	¾ cup	=	6 fl oz	=	180 ml		
		16 tbls	=	1 cup	=	8 fl oz	=	240 ml		
		1 pt	=	2 cups	=	16 fl oz	=	480 ml		
		1 qt	=	4 cups	=	32 fl oz	=	960 ml		
						33 fl oz	=	1000 ml	=	1 L

USEFUL EQUIVALENTS FOR COOKING/OVEN TEMPERATURES

	Fahrenheit	Celsius	Gas Mark
Freeze Water	32° F	0° C	
Room Temperature	68° F	20° C	
Boil Water	212° F	100° C	
Bake	325° F	160° C	3
	350° F	180° C	4
	375° F	190° C	5
	400° F	200° C	6
	425° F	220° C	7
	450° F	230° C	8
Broil			Grill

USEFUL EQUIVALENTS FOR DRY INGREDIENTS BY WEIGHT

(To convert ounces to grams, multiply the number of ounces by 30.)

1 oz	=	1⁄16 lb	=	30 g
2 oz	=	¼ lb	=	60 g
4 oz	=	½ lb	=	120 g
8 oz	=	¾ lb	=	240 g
16 oz	=	1 lb	=	480 g

USEFUL EQUIVALENTS LENGTH

(To convert inches to centimeters, multiply the number of inches by 2.5.)

1 in =				2.5 cm		
6 in =	½ ft =			15 cm		
12 in =	1 ft =			30 cm		
36 in =	3 ft	= 1 yd	=	90 cm		
40 in =				100 cm	=	1 m

THE GOOD HOUSEKEEPING TRIPLE-TEST PROMISE

At *Good Housekeeping*, we want to make sure that every recipe we print works in any oven, with any brand of ingredient, no matter what. That's why, in our test kitchens at the **Good Housekeeping Research Institute**, we go all out: We test each recipe at least three times—and, often, several more times after that.

When a recipe is first developed, one member of our team prepares the dish and we judge it on these criteria: It must be **delicious, family-friendly, healthy,** and **easy to make.**

1 The recipe is then tested several more times to fine-tune the flavor and ease of preparation, always by the same team member, using the same equipment.

2 Next, another team member follows the recipe as written, **varying the brands of ingredients** and **kinds of equipment.** Even the types of stoves we use are changed.

3 A third team member repeats the whole process **using yet another set of equipment** and **alternative ingredients.** By the time the recipes appear on these pages, they are guaranteed to work in any kitchen, including yours. **WE PROMISE.**